Darkening Blackness

Darkening Blackness

Race, Gender, Class, and Pessimism in 21st-Century Black Thought

Norman Ajari

Translated by Matthew B. Smith

polity

Originally published in French as *Noirceur. Race, genre, classe et pessimisme dans la pensée africaine-américaine au XXIe siècle* © Éditions Divergences, 2022

This work received support for excellence in publication and translation from Albertine Translation, a program created by Villa Albertine and funded by FACE Foundation.

Polity Press
65 Bridge Street
Cambridge CB2 1UR, UK

Polity Press
111 River Street
Hoboken, NJ 07030, USA

ISBN-13: 978-1-5095-5499-7 (hardback)
ISBN-13: 978-1-5095-5500-0 (paperback)

A catalogue record for this book is available from the British Library.

Library of Congress Control Number: 2023932768

Typeset in 11 on 13pt Sabon
by Fakenham Prepress Solutions, Fakenham, Norfolk NR21 8NL
Printed and bound in the UK by CPI Group (UK) Ltd, Croydon

For further information on Polity, visit our website:
politybooks.com

Contents

Introduction
Centrality and Erasure of Black Pessimism

A specter haunts the Western university: the specter of Critical Race Theory (CRT). Politicians and pundits of both old Europe and the New World have formed a holy alliance to ward off this specter. President Trump and President Macron, Fox News and *Le Monde*, French republicans and conservative Brits agree on its danger. Everywhere, CRT has been deemed a public enemy, charged with corrupting our youth and derailing the pursuit of knowledge. In an increasing number of places throughout the Western world, a concerted and unrelenting attack is being led against scholars whose research deals with race.

Critical Race Theory as Public Enemy

The reaction against CRT has been the most spectacular in the United States: on September 4, 2020, the director of the Office of Management and Budget, Russell Vought, issued a memorandum vilifying racial sensitivity workshops that "trained" government workers "to believe divisive, anti-American propaganda."[1] Following President Trump's time in office, this conservative lawyer founded the Center for Renewing America, a think tank whose primary aim is to fight against "radical philosophy, rooted in Marxism, known as Critical Race Theory," arguing that "where Karl Marx separated society into the capitalist bourgeoisie and the oppressed proletariat, adherents of Critical Race Theory have substituted race for Marx's class and economic distinctions." Hence, they must put a stop to "state sanctioned racism by progressive ideologues," whose intention is "to corrupt children and future generations into both self-loathing and hatred toward their fellow countrymen."[2]

But, before becoming a citizen activist after his party was voted out of office, Vought had managed to convince the head of state of the merits of his crusade. On September 22, 2020, President Trump issued an executive order prohibiting all federal contractors from conducting trainings that address race and gender. The aim of the order was to "combat offensive and anti-American race and sex stereotyping and scapegoating."[3] As is often the case in North America, religious crusades had laid the groundwork for this political directive. Already in 2019, at the conclusion of its annual meeting, the Southern Baptist Convention had issued a more measured, yet no less firm, condemnation of CRT. Meeting resistance within its ranks, particularly from African American pastors and congregants, the largest Protestant congregation in the United States has since hardened its stance on the issue.

In March 2021, a few months after taking office, President Joe Biden rescinded his predecessor's executive order, but the definition of CRT as a pernicious effort to corrupt youth had already become a central talking point of conservative discourse in the United States. In states such as North Carolina, Idaho, and Rhode Island, Republican governors took measures to ban CRT from the curricula of public schools: "The federal government has also been targeted. In May [2021], about 30 Republican elected officials in the House of Representatives introduced a bill, explicitly titled the Stop CRT Act, to ban 'racial equality and diversity training' for federal employees."[4] In a country that has given pride of place to the right of free speech in its most sacred text – it is right there in the first article of the Bill of Rights – these bans had to resort to a rhetoric of exception: the CRT was thus equated with totalitarian speech, making its exclusion from the public arena a matter of national security.

In October 2020, a month after Trump's executive order was issued, British conservatives followed suit. After a debate on Black History Month, the Parliamentary Under-Secretary of State for Equalities, Kemi Badenoch, stated that "any school which teaches these elements of critical race theory, or which promotes partisan political views such as defunding the police without offering a balanced treatment of opposing views, is breaking the law."[5] CRT is well established in the US academy where it originated, although it is not nearly as ubiquitous as the number and prominence of its critics would suggest. Before teaching Black Studies at Edinburgh, I had been recruited in 2019 by Villanova's philosophy department to hold an assistant professor position in Critical Race Theory. In the UK, on the other hand, the discipline occupies a more marginal place, although, as the sociologist of education Paul Warmington has pointed out, the UK has a strong tradition of Black intellectuals whose legacy falls easily in line with the CRT project. Warmington hopes, in the spirit of Pan-Africanism, that the American school and the British school will come together to breed a new generation of Black public intellectuals.[6] This is precisely what the conservative government is trying to prevent – as seen with Kemi Badenoch's pre-emptive strikes – at a time when the murder of George Floyd has incited Black people in the UK to revolt and speak out, driving tens of thousands of demonstrators into the streets.

In France, attacks on race studies were launched on their own terms, and didn't wait for Trump's orders to gain considerable traction in the press – though international conservative solidarity undeniably bolstered this hostility as soon as Donald Trump and Boris Johnson appeared unexpectedly as allies. In January 2018, the far-right monthly *Causeur* published an issue titled "Toulouse 2: the university colonized by *indigénistes.*" In French mediaspeak, *indigénisme*[7] refers to the political program of the radical anti-racist organization Indigènes de la République; it would hence become one of the code names of a French-styled CRT, used pejoratively alongside other neologisms such as *décolonialisme* or *racialisme*. In the French pamphleteer tradition, the mere addition of the suffix *-ism* is thought to make a term instantly reproachable. This issue of *Causeur* may not have been the first of its kind, but it stands out clearly to me for personal reasons. At the time I was teaching at the University of Toulouse, my alma mater, and one of the articles singled me out as one of the university's "colonizers." The article made no effort to hide its white supremacist political agenda. If there were any doubt, one need only glance at the racist caricatures from another article by the same author in the same issue: "It's a cliché but it's true: the individual doesn't exist in African culture, only the group, which subsumes the identity of each individual. It makes sense, then, that philosophy that teaches people 'to think for themselves' is seen as a threat."[8] Seeing, to her dismay, that the philosophy department at the University of Toulouse was holding colloquia and offering courses where Africans and Afrodescendants were making a point of thinking for themselves, this journalist's first reflex was to call for a stop to what she thought was impossible. In fact, she was the one who viewed the act of thinking – especially when coming from Black people – as a threat. In her own intellectual bubble, thank God, she is safe.

By the end of 2018, the fear of race studies had infected the main media outlets of the right, the center, and the left. A highly publicized op-ed entitled "'Decolonialism': a hegemonic strategy," signed by 80 intellectuals, appeared at the end of November in the conservative weekly *Le Point*. The same week, the center left weekly *L'Obs* published an in-depth investigation with the headline "Universities besieged by the 'decolonialists'." In December 2018, in *Libération*, a reputedly left-wing daily, the influential columnist Laurent Joffrin penned an op-ed with the title "The racialized left." The question of race had visibly brought the far right and the left together in what they took to be an affront on their shared values. Since then, this kind of "reporting," along with a wide array of think pieces, became de rigueur in the French press, commanding an increasing amount of space in the newspapers. The inevitable spread of this discourse ended up reaching the executive power. In June 2020, speaking with *Le Monde*, President Macron took issue with French academics guilty of "dividing the Republic."⁹ The Trump effect was in full force in February 2021 when Frédérique Vidal, the Minister of Higher Education, deploring what she saw as a mix of Chairman Mao and Ayatollah Khomeini among French scholars, used her position to authorize an investigation into "Islamo-leftism" within the French academy.

This book examines the pessimism of contemporary African American theory. For it is precisely this, its pessimism, that provokes the most outspoken and vehement critiques of this academic discourse in the press and political arena. This is what is behind the attempts to ban CRT. As Reverend Michael Wilhite, pastor of New Hope Baptist Church in Newtonville,

Indiana, put it: "It's just the opposite of the gospel. Under critical race theory, there is no hope. If you're white, you're automatically a racist because of white supremacy. But with the gospel there's hope."[10] Both Trump's executive order and its various iterations imposed by a handful of American states to legitimize the censorship of CRT share the same philosophy: they must combat the belief that white people and public institutions in the United States are inherently prone to racism. Similarly, journalists, columnists, and French politicians simply refuse to accept that some view the French Republic as a project devoid of future prospects for minorities. Fundamentally, the principal authors of CRT express disillusionment, disaffection, even hostility toward liberal democracy and the State. As one of its leading contemporary scholars, the African American philosopher Tommy Curry, explains:

> It has come as a great surprise to whites that the Black scholars that have informed Critical Race Theory do not believe in the promises of Western democracy or the delusion that racial equality is possible in these white democratic societies. Since the nineteenth century, Black scholars have insisted upon the permanence of white racism in the U.S. and other white empires. Contrary to the academic depictions of Black American figures as hopeful and invested in the democratic experiment of America, Black thinkers insisted that anti-Blackness stains Black Americans into perpetuity. Throughout the 1800s, historic Black figures associated Black liberation with (the Haitian) revolution not incorporation in the U.S. In America and Europe, the liberal democratic ideal insists that the "race problem" between Blacks and whites will inevitably be resolved with the passing of more time. This idea of automatic progress insists that the death and dying of Black people – while constant – slowly moves white populations towards greater social consciousness and racial understanding.

This optimism regarding anti-Black racism, or the set of racial antipathies wedding Blackness and Africanity to inferiority, savagery, and disposability, depends ultimately on the ability of white democracies to manage the outrage and political dissent Black American and European populations have to their disproportionate deaths, disadvantage, and poverty compared to the white citizenry.[11]

For critics of CRT or decolonial thought, this pro-Black pessimism, which views the State and white civil society as intrinsically unjust institutions, must be stopped before it spreads. The official narrative has it that the American and French Republics, as well as the United Kingdom, are constantly driven by reform and progress for minorities. We are told that slavery, colonialism, imperialism, and segregation are all ancient history – not that they have merely metamorphosed to preserve the structure of inequality. Any theory that frames state optimism as a vehicle for perpetuating subjugation and alienation under the banner of democracy should thus be squashed by government forces. To modify a famous quote from the South African Steve Biko, we might say the most powerful weapon in the hands of the oppressor has become the *hope* of the oppressed. This hope blunts critiques of structural or state racism, as it interprets this racism as stages, fleeting moments, which call for reformist patience rather than radical action. But refusing to place hope in the master, the colonizer, the exploiter is what allows one to regain confidence in one's own dignity and strength. All three great imperial nations share the fear that Black people, and other people of color, will stop seeing them as places of progress toward justice, equality, and tolerance, and instead come to recognize them as state regimes fundamentally defined by a dehumanizing racism.

Pessimism as the Cornerstone of the Black Radical Tradition

This book focuses on two contemporary currents within African American thought: Afropessimism and Black Male Studies. Although they offer novel concepts and interpretations, they both return to a classical orientation within the history of Afro-diasporic thought. I began by discussing the attacks on CRT and decolonial thought in the US, France, and Britain in recent years. A parallel can be drawn between these attacks and those on Afropessimism and Black Male Studies in some academic and activist circles. The latter attacks accuse these currents of sowing distrust of institutions from countries once tied to Black slavery, of casting doubt on the benefits or promises these institutions purport to offer us, or of engendering a Black separatism that is by necessity toxic and patriarchal.

Behind these accusations is the belief that Afropessimism and Black Male Studies mark a departure from – or even are a betrayal of – Black political thought. These criticisms follow a consistent pattern. Over the past 30 years, the struggles, ideas, and achievements of the Black radical tradition have been subjected to a historical revisionism in accordance with the political sensibilities of an era from which the Black Power Movement has all but vanished. This is symptomatic of the collective neglect of the history of Black liberation politics and theories, which can be seen within Black Studies itself. To be sure, the works of Black writers such as Frank Wilderson, Jared Sexton, David Marriott, or Tommy Curry began appearing only over the last 20 years or so, but their works fall squarely in line with an essential component of Black radical thought since at least the Haitian Revolution – namely, that of Black pessimism. I am using this matter-of-fact designation to refer to the idea that racism or anti-Blackness are pillars of both white states and white civil societies. It follows that Black liberation requires breaking free from these structures – a step which is often conceived as the first to take to lead to their abolishment. As opposed to an integrationist or reformist approach, Black pessimists see anti-Blackness as intrinsic to modern European civilization – not as a contingent ideological apparatus in the service of capitalist exploitation or other forms of social violence.

Jean-Jacques Dessalines, the victorious general of the Haitian Revolution, is without doubt one of the first great figures of this Black pessimism. He was convinced that the best way to unite all Haitians of African descent, whether they were previously free or slaves, was to take revenge against the French and engage in an endless fight. As he declared on April 28, 1804:

> At last the hour of vengeance has struck, and the implacable enemies of human rights have suffered punishment for their crimes. ... I saw two classes of men born to love each other, to help each other, which blended together and became almost indistinguishable, driven by vengeance to strike, with honor, the first blows. Blacks and yellows [i.e. mulattoes], long divided by the wily duplicity of the Europeans, you who today are but one whole, one family, have no doubt, your perfect reconciliation needed to be sealed with the blood of our executioners.[12]

Dessalines's logic was a radical reversal of the logic of the Haitian colonial system, which, as Baron de Vastey explained, was based on white domination and the massacre or enslavement of Blacks.[13]

Reversal here shouldn't be confused with a simple vendetta. What Dessalines was after was a more profound, *ontological* upheaval. Under slavery, whites defined their humanity against Black slaves and mulattoes. The latter were seen as a vile and worthless mass that threw into relief, by way of contrast, white supremacy. Shipload after shipload of Black bodies were needed to provide the colony not only with a new labor force, but with the raw material for white self-assertion. With the reversal led by Dessalines, Blacks rose to the foreground. To form and unite the Black community in Haiti – that is, to humanize collectively the former slaves and segregated people of color – the morbid relationship between whites and Blacks need not be maintained as it was during the slave era. Rather, the white gaze must simply cease to exist. The first modern Black political community has as its condition of possibility a violent withdrawal from all interaction with Europeans. This is perhaps the clearest and most radical expression of Black pessimism. And it is precisely this expression that is found in the most important Black writers of the twentieth century.

W. E. B. Du Bois, an African American thinker praised for his book *The Souls of Black Folk*, is a case in point. Although he is generally understood as fully committed to the American democratic ideal, as someone who believed the destiny of Black people is to find their place within, and contribute to, this ideal, it is often forgotten that, in the 1930s, he later rejected this idealization of African Americans as torchbearers of European political ambitions. Indeed, he became increasingly skeptical of the supposed virtues of integrationism, which led him to leave the NAACP (The National Association for the Advancement of Colored People), a major organization behind the Civil Rights struggle which he had helped to found. In an article published in *The Crisis* in 1933, he wrote: "There seems no hope that America in our day will yield in its color or race hatred any substantial ground and we have no physical nor economic power, nor any alliance with other social or economic classes that will force compliance with decent civilized ideals in

Church, State, industry or art."[14] Even going so far as to reverse his negative stance against Marcus Garvey, Du Bois now saw the construction of political autonomy and social self-determination as the path to African American liberation.

At the same time, on the other side of the Atlantic, a group of young French-speaking colonial subjects were forging an intellectual and literary avant-garde movement called Négritude that would have a profound impact on the history of Africana thought. Its driving force was the rejection of the imperial horizon of assimilation and its attendant disdain of African and West Indian cultures. The notion of Négritude appeared for the first time in 1935 in the second issue of *L'Étudiant noir*, a review for which Aimé Césaire served as lead editor. In a piece entitled "Nègrerie: racial consciousness and social revolution," Césaire defended a Black revolutionary politics delivered from the temptation to imitate white communism and the politics of the French left: "To be revolutionary is all good and well, but insufficient for us blacks [*nègres*]; we must not be revolutionaries that just happen to be black [*noirs*], but properly revolutionary blacks [*nègres révolutionnaires*] ... For the Revolution, let us claim ownership over ourselves, towering above official white culture, looking down on the 'intellectual rigging' of a conqueror's imperialism."[15] Many other political and intellectual figures could be cited to illustrate the long history of this theoretical position, since pessimism regarding the emancipatory promises of white institutions runs through Black radical activism and political philosophy. For more than two centuries, the Black movement has not defined itself through its pursuit of allies and partnerships based on its shared interests with other social groups. Although this is how it is often presented today, the Black movement has thrived by constantly affirming Black specificity while pursuing autonomy, even sovereignty.

However, a shift did occur in the theoretical and political discourse on Blackness. In his 1984 book *The Myth of Black Progress*, African American sociologist Alphonso Pinkney expressed concern over the coincidence of an increasingly pervasive discourse of optimism regarding the Black condition throughout the United States and the dismantling of Black radical political activism of the 1960s and 1970s: "There appears to be, on the part of some social scientists, a curious need to convey the impression that American society is a progressive one on matters of human rights for black people. Distorted statistics and erroneous data are often used to support this myth. Yet there is overwhelming evidence to the contrary."[16] In recent decades, intersectional feminism as well as certain liberal trends within Africana philosophy have been important vectors for the spread of this myth within the academy. These same forces have served to undermine the centrality of Black pessimism to our intellectual and political history.

The way the Black radical tradition, Pan-Africanism, and Black nationalism have been re-interpreted in the field of African American political philosophy over the past 20 years is telling. For the African American philosopher Tommie Shelby, unless these can be married to the sort of political liberalism championed by John Rawls, they are irrelevant to our present moment.[17] Although his thinking diverges from that of Shelby's on some key points, especially on the place of Rawls' thinking in regard to Black nationalism and racial justice, the Jamaican philosopher Charles Mills also embraces political liberalism as the ultimate goal of Black social critique. Hence his notion of "Black radical liberalism." In recent decades, debates about Black nationalism and radicalism have gradually morphed into intra-party quarrels about liberalism, as if no other political horizon were conceivable.

Black feminism had already paved the way for this dismissal of the Black radical tradition. Lambasting the patriarchal, chauvinistic, and backward nature of the Black movement, the founding figures of Black feminism – such as Michele Wallace, bell hooks, or the Combahee River Collective – staked a position more in keeping with European feminism and in line with the status quo. Adopting a generic European feminist framework while drawing on the language and identity-based posture of Black radicalism, this Black feminism created an intellectual hybrid at odds with – if not heretical to – the Black Power Movement. And Black feminism is often seen today as the culmination of the Black movement. But its most influential positions derive from a radical rejection of this legacy and an outright hostility to Black pessimism. Instead, it is a doctrine of hope, of coalition-building, crystalized today in the ubiquitous term "intersectionality." It might be worth asking whether Black feminism is the offspring of the Black integrationists of the 1960s, such as Roy Wilkins or George Schuyler, whose hostility toward Black radical organizations knew no bounds. Ill-founded accusations of sexism directed at the Black Power Movement in the 1980s conveniently recall and reinforce accusations of racism, fascism, and even Black Hitlerism made by Wilkins and Schuyler 20 years earlier.

Black thought in recent decades has been defined in large part by this suppression of its own history, opting instead for an ill-considered place within liberal ideology where the question of Black self-determination cannot even be posed, much less pursued. Since the 1980s, the Black radical tradition has virtually been at a standstill, with the theory and politics of Black Power all but abandoned. Compare this to Marxism, which, despite being marginalized for a time after the fall of the Soviet Union, has continued to be at the center of discussions and debates, adapting to the challenges of the time. Amid this grim setting, Black Male Studies and Afropessimism have emerged like the return of the repressed. After the Black movements of the twentieth century suffered the trauma of state repression, Black thought sought refuge on the safer shores of liberalism and intersectionality. However, now that questions of mass incarceration, police violence, crippling debt, or social precarity are more relevant to Black communities than ever before, the dominant forms of African American critical theory have proven less equipped to address these matters than various strands of Black pessimism of the last century. The resurgence of these arguments restores a forgotten continuity. This book explores the re-emergence of this long-neglected theoretical space and describes its potential for illuminating a set of problems with newfound relevance.

Often caricatured as backward-looking, chauvinistic, misogynistic, or reactionary, theories informed by Black nationalism, Pan-Africanism, or Black radicalism have gradually lost ground to more liberal discourses that align closely with the dominant trends of the preponderantly white humanities. But these major currents of twentieth-century Black thought are re-emerging in a new form, with new insights and emotional registers. Pessimism, once a mere feature of Black radicalism, is now core to its approach. This pessimism has never been directed at Black people – their qualities, their courage – but rather at white society's ability to overcome its own anti-Black hatred. Hence the recourse, throughout the twentieth century, to projects such as the return to Africa or the founding of a Black nation in North America, among others. According to the philosopher Cornel West:

> the pessimism on which black nationalism was predicated was never fully embraced in an organizational sense. Black people usually still maintain some

possibility for a multiracial coalition, for trying to extend the scope of democracy in America. I think the role of the black church has been crucial in this, because what it has done historically is steal the thunder from black nationalism. It highlights black cultural distinctiveness and, despite calling for group cohesiveness, its message is universalistic.[18]

To be sure, the history of Black nationalism and the Black church cannot be disentangled. Henry M. Turner, Bishop of the African Methodist Episcopal Church, was one of the strongest advocates of the return to Africa solution in the late nineteenth century, but he had few followers.[19] Despite some recent attempts to frame its discourse in more radical terms, as did Black liberation theology in the 1960s, the Black church has largely become a powerful instrument in maintaining the status quo. Its theology of prosperity that sanctifies personal enrichment and a life of luxury, its social conservatism, and its embrace of establishment politics underlie its universalist message. While the political ambitions of Bishop Turner are absent from contemporary debates, the distrust of institutions remains strong, and there has been an erosion of faith in the supposed benefits of a multiracial coalition. In the African American context, optimism and pessimism are generally a function of one's feelings about the possibility of assimilation in a predominantly white society. Often, the optimists are considered liberal, and the pessimists radical. In other words, optimists believe Black people may see their humanity fully recognized, whereas the pessimists consider anti-Blackness to be a cornerstone of the current world order. For the latter, anti-Blackness can only be defeated by overthrowing this world order. Hence the urgency of reimagining Black thought and society from the ground up. As an intellectual history-in-the-moment, *Darkening Blackness* documents this return of pessimism in contemporary thought. It comes at a time of bitterness left in the wake of Obama's presidency, at a time of bewilderment caused by the spectacle of Donald Trump's racist harlequinades, at a time when the Black Lives Matter movement has been, by turns, radicalized, consolidated, co-opted.

The aim of *Darkening Blackness* is threefold. First, this work makes a case for two emergent fields of inquiry, within African American studies in academia, that are essential to Black social critique: Afropessimism and Black Male Studies. The goal is to highlight the contributions of these fields in the favorable light offered by a Black radical and Pan-African perspective. This entails identifying the sources and inspirations of these movements, and thus fleshing out their broader history. Second, this work seeks to make use of the tools developed by these fields by analyzing other texts and contexts, principally within a francophone space. And, third, *Darkening Blackness* pursues the aim of my previous work, *Dignity or Death*, to generate a theoretical discourse on Afrodescendants by Afrodescendants themselves. Ultimately, I hope this book, which focuses almost exclusively on the Black condition in the Global North, will appeal to Black readers in Africa, the Caribbean, and beyond. Dialogue, debate, and translation between theoretical perspectives from different diasporas and different regions of the African continent is certainly the most urgent challenge for the future of Black thought – perhaps the only one that really matters.

Chapter Summary

The first chapter sketches a brief intellectual history of Afropessimism, beginning with the origin of the term in an anti-Black Africanist discourse at the end of the twentieth century to its reappropriation in current debates among African American scholars. The figureheads of this movement, Frank Wilderson and Jared Sexton, borrowed conceptual tools from different intellectual traditions. This chapter will discuss three of these traditions. First, CRT, which counters in radical terms the pervasive narrative that sees the progressive democratization of American institutions as the true path to Black emancipation. Second, the thought of the Italian philosopher Giorgio Agamben, whose concept of the "paradigm" is taken up and adapted by Afropessimists to theorize the Black condition, which is interpreted as intrinsically linked to the paradigm of the slave. Defined by overexposure to gratuitous violence, social death, and fungibility, Black people today belong to the same paradigm as slaves before them. Finally, a current of Black feminism embodied by Hortense Spillers and Saidiya Hartman. This current focuses most notably on the dehumanization of Black women, on the incommunicability between white femininity and the Blackness of Black women, and on the white desire that perversely drives anti-Blackness.

The second chapter analyzes the core tenets of Afropessimism. Its intellectual project is built on the idea that the intensity and persistence of anti-Blackness cannot be explained without understanding a deeper anti-Black unconscious. According to Afropessimism, we are caught in a vast economy of desire where others gain immense satisfaction from dominating, instrumentalizing, and humiliating Black lives, to the point of this becoming a criterion of membership in authentic humanity. Anti-Blackness humanizes non-Black people, who also derive pleasure from this experience.

The third chapter springs from a certain dissatisfaction with the way Afropessimism treats gender. My scruples, however, are at odds with the diagnosis of the Black feminist critic Jennifer C. Nash, who, in her assessment of Black Studies, remains "concerned at the host of ways that the dead are always figured as black men, and black women are those who mourn, who grieve, and who make visible black male suffering."[20] In contrast, this chapter explores the reluctance of Afropessimists to problematize Black masculinity and the forms of violence that are connatural to it. Continuing the legacy of CRT, the philosopher Tommy Curry offers a way of doing just this by interrogating the condition of Black men. This chapter examines and contextualizes Curry's critique of the dominant liberalism of current social philosophy and feminist theory, drawing on the theories of his predecessors such as David Marriott and Sylvia Wynter. The respect bestowed upon these fields by the academy today masks their anti-Black leanings.

In the main currents of critical theory, from the nineteenth century to the present, violence has always been considered a phenomenon of contingency. The fourth and final chapter of this book begins with the fact that, for African American theorists of pessimism, contingency fails to explain anti-Black violence. Not all Black people are systematically assaulted, but history has shown us that being Black alone is sufficient reason for being assaulted, even killed. This ontological particularity of the Black condition leads to a strategic conception of politics, which has been taken up most notably by Frank Wilderson. This analytical framework will be used to interrogate three political spaces. First, in the Western context in general, and the United States in particular, I offer a critique of the hegemonic strategy, which sees itself as the only conceivable political strategy. Second, in the Canadian context, I bring the approach of Wilderson and Sexton to bear on the arguments of the Quebec theorist Dalie Giroux to show how the Black question is eclipsed by questions of land and culture. Not uncoincidentally, these questions also foreclose any revolutionary approach. Finally, in a French context, I will give a brief history of the anti-racism political movement. As the presence and the history of the Maghreb occupy a central place in this movement, I hope to shed light on the reasons for, and the consequences of, its centrality. I also highlight areas where the perspective of this movement intersects with and diverges from that of Black pessimists.

1

The Sources of the Afropessimist Paradigm

Poorly understood in French-speaking regions, Afropessimism, a current of Black Studies that has garnered an increasing amount of attention, finds itself today at the center of countless debates and controversies. My goal in this chapter is to outline the principal tenets of this emerging school of thought on Black life, culture, and politics, which, though originating in the academy in the United States, is now spreading beyond its borders. Black Studies began as an interdisciplinary endeavor in the US academy in the 1960s and 1970s. It set out to produce knowledge from the unique perspective of a population that, throughout the modern era, had been considered incapable even of thinking. As the African American historian Manning Marable has written, at the heart of this undisciplined discipline is an unwavering concern for its social relevance. Black Studies abandoned the ideals of objectivism and axiological neutrality as it saw itself lending a voice and a conceptual framework to the interests of the African diaspora: "We cannot be disinterested observers, hiding behind the false mantel of 'scholarly objectivity,' as the physical and spiritual beings of millions of people of color and the poor are collectively crushed."[1] Black Studies sought at the outset to position itself as the proof and the expression of dignity in African diasporic thought.

To be Black is to be a descendant of enslaved or colonized peoples whose very humanity has incessantly been called into question. Black Studies is not a field within the humanities that focuses solely on a specific population, such as Afrodescendants or Africans. It is just the opposite: it concentrates on the *inhumanities*, so to speak. That is, it offers at once a rational discourse on the processes of dehumanization, its mechanics and history, while honoring the discourse of those who speak from the place of a belittled humanity – those who inhabit a body held as abject. As opposed to the traditional form of disciplines in Western universities, Black Studies is not defined by an *object* of study in the same way that law, for example, studies the legal system, or history studies archives, or medicine the disorders of the human body. Black Studies distinguishes itself by taking the Black condition to be a *subject* of knowledge. As a result, Black Studies is by design free to move between disciplines and methodologies.

Even within Black Studies, Afropessimism situated itself at the outset by exposing the limits of European thought. The aim was not to claim white people were intrinsically bound to these limits, but rather to call attention to the gaps and blind spots in the history of thought originating from Europe.

> Afropessimism, then, is less a theory and more of a *metatheory*: a critical project that, by deploying Blackness as a lens of interpretation, interrogates the unspoken, assumptive logic of Marx, postcolonialism, psychoanalysis, and feminism through rigorous theoretical consideration of their *properties and assumptive logic*, such as their foundations, methods, form, and utility; and it does so, again, on a higher level of abstraction than the discourse and methods of the theories it interrogates. ... It is pessimistic about the claims theories of liberation make when these theories try to explain Black suffering or when they analogize Black suffering

with the suffering of other oppressed beings. ... Blacks do not function as political subjects; instead, our flesh and energies are instrumentalized for postcolonial, immigrant, feminist, LGBTQ, transgender, and workers' agendas. ... A Black radical agenda is terrifying to most people on the Left – think Bernie Sanders – because it emanates from a condition of suffering for which there is no imaginable strategy for redress – no narrative of social, political, or national redemption.[2]

For Afropessimists, the Black condition must be understood, treated, theorized from within, not cited as an instance of a wider range of phenomena, metaphors, or analogies by theoretical approaches or political programs for which Blackness is but one issue among many others, buried in a chain of equivalences. This first chapter explores the intellectual context from which Afropessimism emerged. But it also seeks to shed light on what preceded it: the theories that laid the groundwork for its emergence and inspired its development.

The Theoretical Space of Afropessimism

As Greg Thomas reminds us, in a compelling critique of the Afropessimist paradigm, the notion of "Afropessimism" taken up by contemporary Black Studies is a semantically charged term.[3] In the political lexicon of African development, it evokes a view put forth by figures such as the journalist Stephen Smith and the far-right historian Bernard Lugan, among others.[4] In this context, the term "Afropessimism," frequently used with a negative connotation, suggests that sub-Saharan societies are fundamentally incapable of accommodating liberal modernity, democratic institutions, and a market economy. Failing to meet the standards of the modern era, the Black continent is doomed to remain under-developed.

Although this negative understanding of the term prevails today, despite the many assumptions it makes regarding the forward march of history, the need for "development," and the unquestioned acceptance of the Western model, other understandings have also been at play over the past several decades. In 1990, in the context of a Third-Worldist political imaginary that had defined Africa during the previous half-century but had since lost its appeal, the Congolese writer Sony Labou Tansi used the notion to bolster a Pan-African discourse:

> Currently, the tragedy we're drowning in is that Africa thinks little, sells next to nothing, and buys recklessly. The worst part is that we simply call this tragedy "Afropessimism," a term that is excruciatingly inadequate as a justification for the biggest mess of all times. We smile as we let History (which has more than once cuckolded us) make us slaves of a shameful thrill – the mortified thrill of raw materials, prices that condemn us to build and develop broken economies, at the bottom of the cruelest, most unbearable, most inhuman indignity that men can swallow without spitting it back out.[5]

Expressed with flair and concision, Sony Labou Tansi's apocalyptic vision exposes the paradox of the concept, which became increasingly accentuated throughout the course of the twenty-first century. Indeed, Tansi takes a strong position against the discourse he called Afropessimist, which he saw as fatalistic and cynical. He also saw it as a cause of complacency and viewed it as complicit in the dehumanizing and demeaning forces behind Africa's exploitation. And yet, although he refuses to resign himself to this view, his own assessment of Africa isn't without its share of pessimism. He has no choice but to acknowledge the political failure of one-party systems, economic stagnation, and the hopelessness felt by the younger population in Central Africa in the early 1990s. In other words, Sony Labou Tansi doesn't offer a form of "Afro-optimism" in response. His view, too, takes the form of a politicized pessimism.

The recent shift in the term's meaning stems from interrogating anew the causes of the state of misery, dependence, and violence endemic to Africa. Should Africanness itself be held responsible for this – that is, is it a matter of social organization, culture, or race? Or, rather, is it a political, or geopolitical, question tied to imperialism and to what Kwame Nkrumah has called neocolonialism?[6] Despite Tansi's careful assessment, it was the former of these two positions that dominated political discourse for the next decade or so. It wasn't until Saidiya Hartman, an African American literary theorist and historian, reframed the debate in 2003 that a conceptual shift took place. She used the term "Afropessimism" during an interview with Frank Wilderson, who would later take it up in his own work, inflecting its meaning to align with his own philosophy.

Discussing the relationship between Africans and Afrodescendants – that is, the relationship between the traumas from the colonization of Africa and from the transatlantic slave trade, Hartman stated: "When you look at certain African writers, say Achille Mbembe and the other so-called 'Afro-Pessimists' who are diagnosticians of their society, you see the consequences of the colonial project."[7] Hartman thus inherits the category of Afropessimism from the tradition described above. However, she seeks to cast the authors labeled as Afropessimist in a new light, without challenging the categorization itself. As with Sony Labou Tansi, the understanding of Afropessimism that she advances offers a clear-eyed view of the devastation wrought by colonialism and racism. Hartman observes that these historical phenomena have caused an unacknowledged level of destruction and a number of untreated pathologies. The Afropessimists, for her, are those who give an unblinking account of the catastrophe. Eschewing a comforting portrait, they describe this radical devastation in raw and blunt terms.

In the 1990s and 2000s, the concept of Afropessimism was decidedly ambiguous. Make no mistake, it most often suggested a pessimism regarding the future – what could be called a sort of Afro-fatalism: the diagnosis of a forestalled future, with all paths forward definitively cut off. But its pessimistic stance can also be understood as a lucid take on the continuity of violence bequeathed by the history we inhabit. The tension between these two positions is acutely felt in Sony Labou Tansi's text. In this intellectual context, there is not a single coherent Afropessimist discourse whose only counter position would be one of optimism. Confronting these multiple interpretations, Frank Wilderson's strategy was to appropriate the concept and apply it to a new setting: that of the Black diaspora in North America. His Afropessimism aims to provide a penetrating perspective on the Black condition in general.

It is worth dwelling on the forces and figures that make this understanding of Afropessimism possible. The term no longer refers solely to the theories of mostly white intellectuals, whose contempt toward Black people and the Black continent is hardly dissimulated. Rather, it points to a radical school of thought that emerged from within Black Studies in North America. For the sake of clarity, I will focus on three major currents related to this thought, highlighting their principal points of relevance: the social diagnosis of CRT; the methodology of the Italian philosopher Giorgio Agamben; and a particular concern within Black feminism centered on questions of death and dehumanization. Many others could be included, starting with the work of the Martinican Frantz Fanon, whose mix of psychoanalysis, literary analysis, and revolutionary political thought set the tone for Afropessimism at its outset. But to bring to light its singularity, it seems more effective to contrast it with similarly oriented contemporary theories, rather than to go back to older sources of inspiration.

Critical Race Theory

Critical Race Theory is a form of social critique that originated in the field of law in the United States before going on to impact the social sciences, philosophy, and the humanities. Self-proclaimed Afropessimists make no explicit reference to this school of thought, whose empirical approach, informed by the methodology of law, the tools of the social sciences, and the political heritage of the Civil Rights Movement, is at odds with the speculative, psychoanalytical, and aesthetic tendencies of Afropessimism. However, for the philosopher Tommy Curry, these two movements share a similar philosophical orientation, questioning the *doxa* that sees steady progress in the Black condition in North America.[8] In fact, CRT, spearheaded by the lawyer Derrick Bell (1930–2011) in the 1980s, paved the way for Afropessimism by arguing that the United States was beset by "permanent racism." Drawing on different methods and a distinct idiom, CRT made the claim before the Afropessimists that anti-Blackness wasn't only a structural problem, but was integral to the very social organization of the United States.

In 1992, Bell wrote:

> Black people will never gain full equality in this country. Even those Herculean efforts we hail as successful will produce no more than temporary "peaks of progress," short-lived victories that slide into irrelevance as racial patterns adapt in ways that maintain white dominance.

> This is a hard-to-accept fact that all history verifies. We must acknowledge it, not as a sign of submission, but as an act of ultimate defiance.[9]

This is the historical framework that orients Afropessimistic philosophical speculation, a framework that, importantly, contests the grand narrative of Black emancipation. For Bell, who lent his legal skills to the Civil Rights Movement, this analysis also offers a bitter assessment of its achievements. It stems from a diagnosis of a period when "the continuing devastation of racial discrimination is minimized, even ignored, while we in the civil rights movement who gained some renown as we labored to end those injustices are conveniently converted into cultural reinforcements of the racial status quo."[10] In short, for Bell, the quasi-beatification of certain prominent figures of anti-racist activism, such as Martin Luther King Jr., conveys that their objectives were achieved.

The nation celebrates these activists as though they accomplished all of their goals, as though their political projects have actually come to fruition and the state has been reshaped to meet their demands. In reality, most of their efforts ended in failure and society remains fundamentally unchanged. In Bell's view, US lawmakers have always sacrificed Black aspirations for the benefit of whites, redressing injustices only when it served to preserve the status quo, that is, when it came at no cost to the interests of white people. In other words, "social advances" for Black people have only occurred in those rare moments when their interests aligned with those of white elites.

An example will serve to illustrate the unresolvable contradiction that CRT exposes. The election of Black figures to major city halls across the nation in the 1960s and 1970s was clearly an effect of riots and protests that took place in cities nationwide (notably the riots provoked by the assassination of Martin Luther King in 1968). But the election of this new generation of African American leaders would be unthinkable if it didn't directly benefit the Democratic Party, which, at the time, struggled to address racially charged issues, especially the riots. These new faces solidified the progressive party's popularity in majority Black regions and helped to bolster a new Black middle class – all without sacrificing the dominance of the white democratic *nomenklatura*. This history demonstrates how the more or less avowed convergence of interests between whites and Blacks can lead to notable social changes that are often unilaterally viewed as advances toward Black emancipation. What's more, these supposed advances are often met with significant backlash, which targets not only Black people but other oppressed populations as well. Such is the case with affirmative action, which leads some to question the legitimacy of its beneficiaries while, at the same time, often negatively impacts access to higher education for the white working-class population.[11] Thus, the white middle and upper classes are largely unaffected by this policy, which is designed to address the unequal distribution of wealth and social privilege.

Any dream of attaining equality in the United States is crushed under Bell's "racial realism." Even with improved standards of living for the general population and the existence of new civil rights, racial inequality remains unchanged. In the United States, white people make up 64% of the population, but hold 88% of its wealth. In contrast, Black people represent 13% of the population and possess only 2.7% of its total wealth.[12] For CRT, social gains hinge on the compassion or permission of a dominant white majority – and they can be revoked at any time.[13] And yet, Bell isn't fatalistic. He sees the political fight against racial violence as urgent and necessary. He believes it gives Black existence a renewed sense of purpose and meaning while paving the way for new creative outlets. Make no mistake, the "work and sacrifice, as important as they are, have never been sufficient to gain blacks more than grudging acceptance as individuals."[14] But the political fight makes the success of individuals possible, which, to a limited extent, can also benefit the community.

Giorgio Agamben's Paradigmatic Ontology

Self-proclaimed Afropessimists and those who have been inspired by Afropessimism speak of the Black condition as a sort of *paradigm*. The concept is borrowed directly from the Italian philosopher Giorgio Agamben.[15] In Agamben, paradigms function as meta-concepts. Indeed, his thinking emerges from a methodological framework built on paradigms. Throughout the nine works of his *Homo sacer* cycle, he advances a constellation of notions – some expressed more lucidly than others – that interrogate the relationship between life and various forms of power from a variety of angles. Although his philosophy is indebted to Michel Foucault's work on biopolitics, governmentality, and the technologies of the self, Agamben sets himself apart by favoring a transhistorical interpretation over Foucault's historical periodization and contextualization. He may see himself as merely extending and complementing Foucault's work,[16] but the lineage between their respective approaches is not so clear-cut. Here is how he situates his own theoretical concepts, many of which have become cornerstones of contemporary critical theory:

> *Homo sacer* and the concentration camp, the *Muselmann* and the state of exception, and, more recently, the Trinitarian *oikonomia* and acclamations

are not hypotheses through which I intended to explain modernity by tracing it back to something like a cause or historical origin. On the contrary, as their very multiplicity might have signaled, each time it was a matter of paradigms whose aim was to make intelligible series of phenomena whose kinship had eluded or could elude the historian's gaze.[17]

The notion of the "paradigm," which is taken up in the same terms by Afropessimists, speaks clearly to Agamben's ambitions and approach. It combines Thomas S. Kuhn's epistemology and the notion of *Pathosformeln* articulated by the art historian Aby Warburg: "hybrids of archetype and phenomena, first-timeness (*primavoltità*) and repetition."[18] A paradigm, in this reading, is a singular image or concept that travels freely beyond its sociohistorical place of origin, which is held as contingent, without suffering any significant changes. Agamben borrows Warburg's approach by which "the interpretation of a historical problem also show[s] itself as a 'diagnosis of Western man' in his battle to overcome his own contradictions and to find his vital dwelling place between the old and the new."[19] Hence, if the *Homo sacer*, this man condemned to be killed without consequence, is a product of Roman law, he is also, in equal measure, an emblem of the contemporary era: despite being first described and articulated in Latin, he is not attached to any specific period, not even to his supposed place of origin. The paradigm abolishes the difference between the general and the particular: it creates a link between singularities, indifferent to spatio-temporal norms. The paradigm is an *exemplar* of a general rule that cannot be formulated a priori.[20]

Moreover, in Agamben's work, methodology is of singular importance. It is taken to arise from a deeper, and – to use one of his key words – more essential, urgency. According to Agamben, "the intelligibility in question in the paradigm has an ontological character. It refers not to the cognitive relation between subject and object but to being. There is, then, a paradigmatic ontology."[21] For Agamben, biopower is bound to no specific period. This stands in stark contrast to Foucault's use of the term, which is situated in direct relation to the bourgeois obsession with hygiene in the nineteenth century. In Agamben, the contemporary era is defined by the expansion of biopolitical control over all forms of social organization. The sacralization of human life testifies to this same expansion. And, insofar as it represents a form of life par excellence, it signals an evacuation of politics.

More specifically, Agamben sees the dominance of biopower as that which transforms humans into *Homo sacer* and political life into "bare life" – that is, to use the terms he borrows from Aristotle and his scholastic followers, from *bios politikos* to *zoē*, to animal life. "There is politics because man is the living being who, in language, separates and opposes himself to his own bare life and, at the same time, maintains himself in relation to that bare life in an inclusive exclusion."[22] Man alone can situate himself, in his own life, in direct relation to what is and what should not be; man is capable of saying, for example, that he lives differently from a pig – that his life is incommensurable with that of a pig. Language gives him his place by excluding him from bare life, which, however, continues to express itself as though in the negative. The contradiction performed by taking up politics through language thus situates the living being in permanent relation to bare life. Whereas *bios* is language, *zoē* is only a voice, or a scream.

Bare life is inaugurated not by coming into language, but by being captured by the law. The *Declaration of the Rights of Man and of the Citizen* from 1789

illustrates this – one enters into political life upon birth
(note that the word *nation* derives etymologically from
the Latin word for *birth*): "The principle of nativity and
the principle of sovereignty, which were separated in the
ancien régime (where birth marked only the emergence
of a *sujet*, a subject), are now irrevocably united in the
body of the 'sovereign subject' so that the foundation
of the new nation-state may be constituted."[23] This
submission to the law henceforth abolishes the possibility of free life. This is why "in the political order
of the nation-state ..., the status of refugee has always
been considered a temporary condition that ought to
lead either to naturalization or to repatriation. A stable
statute for the human in itself is inconceivable in the
law of the nation-state."[24] There exists nothing but a
generalized state of exception where the boundaries
between life and law are blurred and all lives are bare
lives – lives separated from any real agency. In the
tradition of Roman law, juridical norms could only
refer to life through some mediated distance – that is,
by creating an abstract juridic personality.[25] Law can
capture life only insofar as it simultaneously pushes it
away, renders it abstract, objectifies it, or introduces
a separation. With individuals seen as separated from
the entirety of what makes their existence singular, the
Homo sacer series can be read as a pointed critique of
separation.[26]

Thus, according to Agamben, the problem of
biopower has to do with a shift in the concept of
life itself: the translation from a political meaning (*la
vita activa*, life in language) to a biological meaning
("bare life," the remainder of a life captured by law).
Many theorists, likely misled by the unhappy term
"bare life," often misinterpret this concept.[27] It cannot
be interpreted literally, as "bare life" doesn't mean
"nothing but life." Rather, it means life separated from
its potential forms, from its ability to project itself into

the future while forever remaining bound to the law through a relationship of sovereignty and to the dictates of an inclusive exclusion. Bare life isn't abandoned to fend for itself, but rather remains at all times subjugated to the State and its various forms of surveillance, control, and punishment. This lies behind Agamben's radical – and at times extremist – anti-Statism, with his opposition to any health measures adopted during the Covid-19 epidemic being a case in point.[28]

Afropessimists mobilize Agamben's notion of the paradigm to offer a critique of anti-Blackness. Their transhistorical and ontological approach, made possible by Agamben's work, represents a clear point of departure from Derrick Bell's historical and empirically grounded approach. Bell's racial realism and his argument concerning the permanence of racism paved the way for the Afropessimist idea according to which the Black slave embodies a paradigmatic figure of violence (a more radical take on the *Homo sacer*). Constructing a paradigm in Agamben's manner can be summarized in three steps. First, identify a singular historical object. Then, identify the governing principles that define it. Finally, trace these isolated features across various historical periods without any concern for their genealogy, lineage, or any other matter related to a linear and chronological history. The governing principles that define the figures or objects are of crucial importance, as they are what allow for the seamless movement between places and periods; they are, in fact, that which renders the places and periods intelligible.

For Frank Wilderson and Jared Sexton, the *Black slave* stands as the fundamental paradigm in their critical theory. Going back to the three steps for constructing a paradigm, we can witness the governing principles they identify in this figure. To begin, the slave is the object of *gratuitous violence*. To be sure, this violence was not without purpose: the submission of slaves through violence realized a whole series of decisive social functions in the slaveholder's mode of production. Most notably, it facilitated over-exploitation and served as a deterrent to potential revolts. But Wilderson's and Sexton's idea of gratuitous violence doesn't refer so much to purposeless violence, but rather to an excess of violence. Indeed, this violence was forever in excess of its own purported goals and limits. Gratuitous violence thus transcends all forms of functional utility: it is expressed throughout history through the torture of slaves, the lynchings that occurred after abolition, or today through police violence and mass incarceration. The second governing principle in the slave paradigm is the notion of *social death*. Social death refers to the absence of any past or future lineage – what the sociologist Orlando Patterson calls natal alienation.[29] In other words, it is a matter of excluding transmission, heritage, affiliations from the symbolic order. For Jared Sexton, this defines the situation of Black people today, where they are excluded from what is held as essential to Western modernity: "black life is *lived* in social *death*."[30] This means this life is undoubtedly lived, but done so without any impact whatsoever on the general order of things.[31] Finally, the third governing principle, which will receive further treatment below, stems from Black *fungibility* – that is, the fact of being submitted to accumulation, of being exchangeable and replaceable, which characterizes the condition of slaves.

Drawing on Patterson's work, Wilderson's definition of the slave nevertheless moves in a decidedly new direction as questions of labor and production become of secondary importance. Although this aspect plays no small role in the slave's condition, being subjected to forced labor is not fundamentally constitutive of slavery. As countless feminist scholars have shown (such as Silvia Federici, Colette Guillaumin, or Christine Delphy, to name a few), unpaid labor isn't unique to slavery. In many traditions, it is considered the woman's lot as wife, mother, or sister. But it would be unwise to equate the condition of European women and that of African slaves brought by force to the New World. Slaves are defined less by what they do – or what they produce – than by what is done to them, or by the type of sovereignty to which they are subjected.

"The Slave is not a laborer but an anti-Human, a position against which Humanity establishes, maintains, and renews its coherence, its corporeal integrity."[32] The slave is the obscene cornerstone of a pluralist liberal society. In other words, without this abject figure, modern civil society and the modern State would lose their very coherence.[33] A society in which non-Blacks, with all their many differences and singularities, can live together is made possible by the slave, who defines the limits of acceptability and tolerance. The slave's status as non-human embodies and crystalizes the unacceptable, that which civil society must repress or contain in order to express differences without troubling social unity. By way of contrast, Blacks humanize other differences by their own difference. Civil society, as a totality, lacks coherence – it is an accumulation of differences fueled by mutual distrust. The threat of conflict, of *stasis* (in ancient Greek) – that is, of civil war – forever looms. Slaves make these differences tolerable, but they don't function like traditional scapegoats who bear all social violence in a sacrificial manner. Possessing Black slaves makes *jouissance* – in the sense of both pleasure and entitlement – equally available to all non-Blacks. There is no democracy without this right bestowed on all – to contempt, disgust, and hate, mixed with desire. Not being Black is a qualifying feature for becoming a valid representative of the community. Thus, in contrast to Agamben's *Homo sacer*, the slave is fundamentally and radically deprived of all political life. Indeed, the law does not capture the slave upon birth in the same way citizenship imprisons bare life within civil society. The birth of the slave doesn't thrust him into the order of the nation, but into that of goods – that is, that of social death and non-humanity.

Flesh and Fungibility in Black Feminism

Since its origins, the condition of the Black slave has maintained a troubled and underexplored relationship to the question of desire. This question is taken up in the work of Hortense Spillers and Saidiya Hartman. These theorists represent a current of Black feminism that focuses on the dehumanization ushered in by slavery. Their approach to racial slavery calls attention to how reducing African women to marketable goods abolishes gender difference. To describe this, Hartman, drawing explicitly on Spillers' work, turned to the politico-economic concept of *fungibility*. This notion refers to the ownership of a certain kind of merchandise: those that are consumed through use and are replaceable by other goods of the same nature, same quality, and same quantity. Black people reduced to slavery fit this description perfectly. Using the concept of fungibility like this paved the way for Afropessimists.

The transatlantic slave trade was singular in its ability to transform millions of human beings into living merchandise. Spillers reminds us that, in the slave ship, "one is neither female, nor male, as both subjects are taken into account as *quantities*."[34] The amount of space a body occupies in the hold, the ration of food allocated to each slave, the minute calculations of losses and profits relative to the imponderable number of victims lost to illness due to the unsanitary conditions onboard – all of these come to define the very being of Africans as cargo. They didn't exist as people, or even as individuals, but only as quantifiable objects with measurable profits. Theories of Black fungibility thus describe the ontological debasement of Blacks, the negation of their humanity, and their reduction to the status of tools, instruments, and sources of profit, through "the systemic application of geometric, arithmetic, and economic calculations to the enslaved as cargo."[35]

These observations led Spillers to distinguish between the notion of *body*, which applies to people – whose physical integrity is accounted for, whose gender difference is acknowledged, whose humanity is recognized – and the notion of *flesh*, which applies solely to slaves. Thus, racialization and violence reduce the African body to the state of fungible Black flesh: a quantifiable, interchangeable, and mobile mass that is deemed unworthy of the respect accorded to humans – that is, to non-Blacks. Flesh is deprived of all the poetry, of all the aestheticization, that define gender difference in societies throughout history. Filthy beings in rags whose flesh oozes from wounds suffered in the holds of ships do not play in the game of gender: the aesthetic performance of femininity or masculinity is not available to them.

Spillers' and Hartman's expression of Black feminism differs significantly from other important figures within this current. To take an emblematic example, the famous African American feminist bell hooks considers oppression from a wider angle, seeing the Black woman as the victim of both sexism and anti-Black hatred. She thus decries the unresolvable dilemma plaguing Black women since the nineteenth century, who were "asked to choose between a black movement that primarily served the interests of black male patriarchs and a women's movement which primarily served the interests of racist white women."[36] This symmetrical positioning, however, is not sustained in hooks' writing. Indeed, rejecting outright and on every occasion the political legacy of mid-century Black radicalism (Malcolm X, the Black Panthers, etc.) as inherently misogynistic, hooks never goes as far as condemning feminist politics as inherently racist – in spite of the repeat claims and ample proof of an untroubled relation between the first women's rights activists and the patriarchy. In fact, many of these early activists stood side by side with men during the *mission civilisatrice* as they subjugated Black, Amerindian, or Muslim "beasts."[37] hooks delegitimizes the legacy of African American politics while guarding feminism from any claims of racism. Not only did she turn a blind eye to this racism, she sought to remove race from the equation altogether: "Although the focus is on the black female, our struggle for liberation has significance only if it takes place within a feminist movement that has as its fundamental goal the liberation of all people."[38] Whereas a politics centered on Blackness alone would be harmful to women in hooks' eyes, feminism is viewed as benefitting the whole of society.

The philosopher Tommy Curry has convincingly shown how caricatures of Black men as aspiring patriarchs or violent phallocrats abound, by way of implication, in feminist political discourse.[39] This makes Spillers' and Hartman's unconventional approach within Black feminism all the more noteworthy. If hooks can fully embrace a feminist politics with explicit universalizing ambitions, it is because she takes the femininity of Black women as a given, as a fact of life. Following this logic, although some white women are recognized as racist, the bond created between women due to their gender remains unalterable and suggests that all women share a similar set of interests beyond any racial divisions. Black women, in this view, are women who happen to be Black: race is only one – almost incidental – aspect of gender.

Spillers and Hartman offer a striking counterpoint to this view. For Hartman, all the fundamental characteristics that have defined European feminine culture – as well as pre-colonial African femininity – are absent, stripped away, or destroyed by the brutal rule of a plantation and slaveholder economy. The position of women as keepers of the house – what Spillers and Hartman call "domesticity" – is unique to European femininity, and contrasts sharply with the history of women reduced to slavery. As Hartman explains:

> what "woman" designates in the context of captivity is not to be explicated in terms of domesticity or protection but in terms of the disavowed violence of slave law, the sanctity of property and the necessity of absolute submission, the pathologizing of the black body, the restriction of black sentience, the multifarious use of property, and the precarious status of the slave within the public sphere.[40]

Motherhood, just like the marital status of slaves, is fundamentally precarious, as it is overexposed to rape, abduction, and separation due to the resale of one of the members of the pseudo family unit.

In sum, according to this "pessimist" strand of Black feminism, there is no universal "woman" subject. Yet this universalist subject is precisely what underlies the tradition of Black feminism represented by Michele Wallace and bell hooks, for whom sisterhood occupies a decisive place: "Radical groups of women continue our commitment to building sisterhood, of making feminist political solidarity between women an ongoing reality. We continue the work of bonding across race and class."[41] For hooks, neither class nor race stands in the way of sisterhood – nor do they pose any problem to the constitution of a unified female political subject. For her part, Wallace speculates that "a multicultural women's movement is somewhere in the future."[42] In contrast, for Spillers or Hartman, Black women share with Black men the same history of dehumanization, of being reduced to quantifiable and fungible flesh. Their only major point of distinction from men and boys is their subjection to sexual violence and the abject experience of motherhood in a racial context. But when it comes to Black and white women, for Spillers and Hartman, there remains an unsurmountable division. There is no femininity, but several irreducible, and at times antagonistic, femininities, constructed on both sides of the racial division.

Afropessimists owe to this heterodoxic Black feminism its emphasis on the radical dehumanization of Blacks and the notion of fungibility. For Frank Wilderson, these are the paradigmatic features that define the very position of the slave: "The violence-induced fungibility of Blackness allows for its appropriation by White psyches as 'property of enjoyment.'"[43] Wilderson is playing with the two opposing meanings of "to enjoy a good," which, on the one hand, signifies the fact of being entitled to a good, but also can be understood more literally as taking pleasure from a good. By super-imposing these two meanings, he sketches an image of the slave as a living good, designed for the enjoyment of others. It was Hartman who first called attention to the slave's status as a good to which one is entitled – that is, which one can enjoy. To be sure, as Hortense Spillers made clear, the slave trade ravished the body of Africans, reducing it to a state of flesh. The ethno-genesis of the Black diaspora caused by slavery cannot be traced back to a continuity of culture, but rather to that of the flesh. This is the zero degree of the collective poetry and symbolism that marks the birth of new Black populations in the Americas.[44]

However, the slave trade is not solely a site of violence, torture, unbearable humiliation, and unspeakable brutality. It is also a space of white *jouissance*, or enjoyment. Acquiring a slave was meant to be an enchanting experience for the buyer. To this end, everything was done to make the captives desirable. Before being put up for sale, they were primed and done up to attract buyers. Music and dance were means to transform the slaves' suffering, fatigue, and despair into a display of pleasure, even enchantment. Slaves were constantly ordered to appear beautiful, happy, full of vigor.[45] Describing this spectacle, Hartman exposes the kinship between abolitionist – and, more generally, anti-racist – discourse and representations and the deeply entrenched tradition of anti-Blackness. Indeed, the representation of the muscular and commanding Black slave, with his Herculean strength and his indefatigable endurance – often evoked to celebrate the slave's potential triumph over his master – falls in line with his place in the plantation imaginary. In reality, it reinforces a conception of the Black man as a powerful beast of burden, which legitimized and justified his overexploitation. Unbearable living conditions were thus disguised as matters of consent and contentment among slaves.

Hartman shines a light on the white man's odd affinity for the Black body by analyzing the rhetorical strategies used by the abolitionist John Rankin. Describing in meticulous detail the torture endured by slaves, Rankin invites his readers to imagine themselves, or one of their kin, in such a situation. With this substitution, one need no longer show sympathy toward Black people, but rather toward oneself. In so doing, Rankin endorses, or at the very least accepts and attests to, a fundamental impossibility of empathy on the part of white people toward Black people. Black suffering only exists as a grotesque and skillfully dramatized spectacle. And it is always mediated through a comparison with white pain. The suffering of the Black body can only be conceived by imagining that of the white body. But this process never allows slaves to break free from the object position to which they were consigned by the slave trade. They remain prisoners of an economy of desire and affects that reduces them to an object of white *jouissance*. Slave owners enjoy slaves as they do a good; white abolitionists enjoy through slaves the good they claim to be performing. In other words, *the only possible relationship between the white body and the Black body is a relationship of use.*

This line of thinking had a profound impact on the notion of Black fungibility deployed by Afropessimists. In their work, this concept refers not only to the convertibility of Black flesh into currency or the inter-changeability of individuals, but also to a complex set of ways in which white desire instrumentalizes or erases Black bodies. The relationship between race and desire – that is, the libidinal economy of Blackness – is at the heart of their analyses.

2

Theoretical Origins of Afropessimism

The abyss of the Black question strains the limits of the imaginable. Historically, violence against Black populations is singularly widespread, naturalized, and systematic, both on a small scale and on an industrial level, by means developed through slavery, genocide, segregation, colonization, incarceration, and exploitation. But the Black body itself, reduced to a state of exchangeable and dehumanized flesh, has constantly been the object of torture, lynchings, rape, castrations, forced penetration, unwanted pregnancies, and mutilations. As a result, Blackness, as the perpetual object of unrelenting aggressions, the target of unhuman brutality, is understood as disposable. In scale as well as intensity, anti-Blackness offers an unparalleled spectacle of abomination.[1] To understand the urgency of Afropessimist thought, we must come to terms with some of the most prominent features of this anti-Blackness, tracing its history and its impact on our current moment. For it is this accumulation of historical experiences to which Afropessimist thought responds.

Historically, monotheistic traditions have been among the oldest and most influential sources of anti-Blackness. Although none of the three major sacred texts professes it, anti-Black hatred has forever gone hand in hand with the spread of these religions. The story of Cham's, or Ham's, curse, is a telling case in point. The biblical version has it more or less this way: Noah, having drifted off to sleep after becoming drunk, is seen naked by Ham, one of his children. Ham goes to tell his brothers, Shem and Japheth, of what he saw. Filled with shame and refusing to let their curiosity get the best of them, they cover their father's sleeping body without looking at him. When he wakes up and learns about Ham's behavior from his brothers, Noah curses Canaan, Ham's son, who henceforth is to become a "servant of servants unto his brethren" (Genesis 9:25, King James Version). This story would later be used to justify countless acts of anti-Black aggression.

Philo of Alexandria, a Jewish philosopher and contemporary of Jesus, was one of the first scholars to make note of Ham's black color.[2] Later, in the sixth century AD, the rabbinic tradition of the Babylonian Talmud directly linked Ham's supposed black skin to Noah's curse, drawing a parallel between Blackness and servitude, which would subsequently be taken up by Islamic traditions.[3] Christianity further developed and refined what started as a Mediterranean tradition of anti-Blackness: in 1454, Pope Nicholas V authorized the king of Portugal to engage in the slave trade under the pretext of evangelizing Black people. Premodern thought began to equate Blackness to abjection and subjection, which was then amplified and radicalized during the modern period.

The transatlantic slave trade stood as a fundamental negation of Black humanity with immeasurable consequences. As the political theorist Achille Mbembe has called it, it was the first instance of the "repeopling of the Earth."[4] Millions of African men and women were torn from their land and dumped onto the Caribbean islands and continental Americas where the genocide of indigenous peoples had made room for these commodified Black laborers. The history of humanity is defined by population shifts, but never before had the world seen people forcefully displaced to faraway lands on this scale. However, individuals were not being sent away: goods were. Inhumane treatment – abuse, rape, torture – was an integral part of the slave trade. What does it mean for this history to underlie the emergence of civil societies? Plantation societies were founded as a direct refusal of equality, which was not only denied but rendered unimaginable. They were designed for Black people to work, reproduce, and perish within their borders. The very presence of Black people was viewed as transient. The pathogenic nature of post-slavery societies, memorably described by Frantz Fanon in *Black Skin, White Masks*, should therefore not surprise us.

The wealth built on the back of slave labor allowed European empires to conquer sub-Saharan Africa. For W. E. B. Du Bois, this was simply racial slavery by other means: "If the slave cannot be taken from Africa, slavery can be taken to Africa."[5] Stripped of all belongings, exiled on their own ancestral land, imprisoned by "a global consensus that Africa is the location of sentient beings who are outside of global community, who are socially dead,"[6] the Igbos, the Yoruba, the Bantous, the Edos, and so many others learned that they were now Black, and that their life was considered outside the bounds of ethics. Gaining independence may have ended the colonial period on paper but the devastation it initiated raged on. This is because independence never gave birth to sovereign political entities that put the interests of their own people first. Beyond their flags and constitutions, countries such as Angola, Zambia, or the Democratic Republic of Congo, among others, appeared "not [as] nation-states developing national resources, but enclaved mineral-rich patches efficiently exploited by flexible private firms, with security provided on an 'as needed' basis by specialized

corporations while the elite cliques who are nominal
holders of sovereignty certify the industry's legality
and international legitimacy in exchange for a piece of
the action."[7] Structurally excluded from the common
good and considered disposable, populations without
ties to these mineral-rich zones remain abandoned in
territories where officials have no interest in governing
and where the survival of the fittest becomes the de
facto law.

From the north to the south of the African continent,
Black people remain dehumanized under the regime of
the flesh. In Libya, after an imperialist military invasion
left the state in tatters, Black people have once again
been enslaved and the bodies of sub-Saharans are selling
at low prices. In Mauritania, the ancestral tradition
of Black servitude continues despite the government's
half-hearted attempts to curb it.[8] The violence that is
routinely unleashed in South Africa against Congolese
or Nigerian immigrants undeniably stems from the
same source of anti-Black hatred. It expresses itself
through the rejection of the "less evolved" and the
"less developed" folk. In other words, of those whose
Blackness stands out the most. And those who try to
flee their continent that has been ravaged by colonial
powers are harassed by sea patrols. Traversing the
Mediterranean in makeshift rafts, hundreds of thousands
sail off, never to see land again.[9]

While the unceasing anti-Blackness of modern international relations continues to plague the African
continent, the condition of the Black diaspora in the
West doesn't look much better: "Nationwide, African
Americans suffer violence at the hands of police across
the United States at almost twice the rate of Latinos and
nearly four times the rate of whites."[10] As the African
American legal scholar Michelle Alexander has shown,
the United States, the country with the highest incarceration rate in the world, disproportionately imprisons

Black people: "The United States imprisons a larger percentage of its black population than South Africa did at the height of apartheid. In Washington, D.C., our nation's capitol [*sic*], it is estimated that three out of four young black men (and nearly all those in the poorest neighborhoods) can expect to serve time in prison."[11] In Europe, there is a deeply held belief that this kind of racial violence and system-wide anti-Blackness is a product of the United States. They believe that the slave-owning or colonialist nations, such as Belgium, France, or the United Kingdom, never saw the same level of anti-Blackness since Brussels, Paris, and London were so far removed from the Black slaves who were overexploited and beaten to death in the colonies.

The gruesome reality shown by repeat crises belies this reasoning. And the crises are but a pronounced expression of a gruesome daily life pervaded by anti-Black hatred. On February 2, 2016, in Aulnay-sous-Bois, a Parisian *banlieue*, Théo Luhaka was sodomized by a police officer with a baton after being stopped and frisked for no apparent reason. The injuries he suffered left him permanently disabled. On July 19, 2016, in Beaumont-sur-Oise, another Parisian *banlieue*, Adama Traoré was pursued by three officers for no apparent reason. Once they caught him, he was immobilized, with the officers putting the full weight of their bodies on him. He died, handcuffed, a few hours later at the police station. The list goes on. According to a report issued by the Defender of French Rights [*Défenseur des droits français*] in January 2017, young Black and Arab men are 20 times more likely than whites to be stopped by the police. The anthropologist Didier Fassin noted that, in one prison where he did extensive fieldwork, "Black and Arab men represented two thirds of all inmates and even more than three quarters of those under thirty, which constituted half of the incarcerated population."[12] This breakdown of non-white inmates nearly mirrors that of the United States.[13] This "American style" of unequal justice can also be seen in the prison systems of England and Wales.[14] Throughout the world, Black life expectancy is among the lowest of all demographic groups. It is also the demographic group with the poorest access to healthcare, and the group with widespread chronic disease due to a poor diet caused by endemic poverty. Throughout the world, death disrupts and cripples Black lives, constantly dragging them toward the grave.

Political reason is embarrassed by this reality and scrambles to make sense of it, to explain it, to reveal its causes. There is no question money is to be made through this mass criminalization of African Americans. The astronomical fines imposed by police on Black populations represent a veritable racial tax on which the economies of major cities are increasingly dependent.[15] However, as Jackie Wang, an American theorist who has been influenced by Afropessimism, has written, "an analysis of prisons and police that solely focuses on the political economy of punishment would be incomplete. There are gratuitous forms of racialized state violence that are 'irrational' from a market perspective. … Why waste an exorbitant amount of public money on incarcerating non-violent offenders, sometimes for life?"[16] This question of gratuitous violence, which is greater in scale and intensity than State repression, and which underlies all the examples of anti-Blackness that have just been evoked, is at the heart of Afropessimist interrogations.

In Africa, in Europe, in the Americas, Blackness is the unredeemable mark of abjection. Anti-Black hatred even pervades regions of the world with no history of colonial exploitation or slavery of Black people, such as Eastern Europe or East Asia. This disproves the idea that anti-Blackness stems from a political culture founded on racial domination. The picture I have sketched here is that of a world where, for centuries, Blackness has been synonymous with abomination, servitude, misery, superfluity. The few statistics and examples I just provided hardly capture the full story of Black indignity, which, with its almost mesmerizing litany of atrocities, could go on without interruption for days on end. To be clear: this is not a story of Black people failing to take the necessary measures to enter into history, or refusing a seat at the table of world culture. On the contrary, it is the unspeakable account of the extraordinary measures and the Herculean effort taken by non-Blacks – at times aided or imitated by some Black people – to brutalize, exterminate, and enslave Blacks. This relentless effort, this frenetic need to annihilate and humiliate the Black figure – prodded on by "the primal activity of fabulation"[17] – defies all rational explanation.

Afropessimism strives to explain this well-documented state of affairs regarding the poverty, vulnerability, and overexposure to violence and death suffered by Black people throughout the world. It does this by calling attention to the libidinal economy of anti-Blackness. The theory, inspired by Frantz Fanon, holds that there is a pervasive anti-Black collective unconscious. This is what is behind the undeniable forces that drive Black life toward death, though there is an adamant refusal to acknowledge its presence. In an Afropessimist analysis, all these historical examples emerge out of the same paradigm, in the Agambenian sense of the term described in the previous chapter: that of the Black slave. And for Wilderson, white desire for the Black slave is central to the architecture of Western civilization: "By *describing* the ways in which Blacks are barred, ab initio, from Human recognition and incorporation, Afro-pessimism argues that the Human would lose all coherence were it to jettison the violence and libidinal investments of anti-Blackness against which it is able to define its constituent elements."[18] In other words, and as we will see presently, humanity affirms its dignity only by way of contrast with the absolute alterity of Black abjection. The non-Black unconscious creates the conditions of its own humanity by plundering, like a scavenger, the Black corpse.

Blackness beyond the Political

Being Black means being condemned to live and die as another's fantasy. Taking this position, Afropessimism challenges one of the most firmly rooted analytical frameworks in the radical African American tradition, in both academic and activist spheres. This framework depends on the idea that anti-Black racism is essentially a form of political domination. This understanding underlies the analyses of Malcolm X or Black Power militants such as Kwame Ture and Charles Hamilton. In their eyes, colonialism, understood as a vast enterprise designed to dispossess racially targeted populations, is the key to understanding the situation. "America is a colonial power. She has colonized 22 million Afro-Americans by depriving us of first-class citizenship, by depriving us of civil rights, actually by depriving us of human rights."[19] The 1960s was the decade of the decolonization of the African continent. The vocabulary of colonization was thus ubiquitous in political discourse. Black militants used it to describe the conditions of the systemic racism they faced in the United States, expressed through expropriation, disenfranchisement, and discrimination. In this sense, colonialism is synonymous with institutional racism or state racism.[20] The political tradition of Black radicalism is expressed in the academy in the work of the Jamaican philosopher Charles Mills, who urged us to recognize that "racism (or, as I will argue, global white supremacy) is itself a political system, a particular power structure of formal or informal rule, socioeconomic privilege, and norms for the differential distribution of material wealth and opportunities, benefits and burdens, rights and duties."[21]

From Malcolm X to Mills, radical critiques of anti-Black racism generally see racism as a form of politics, be it called "colonialism" or "white supremacy." This political apparatus is depicted as an architecture of inequality that is expressed through laws, the practices of state agents, or administrative decisions made at the expense of the interests of Black populations. Afropessimists don't deny this state of affairs, but they consider politics a secondary matter. They don't claim that political and social displays of anti-Blackness are merely anecdotal or negligible, but that they stem from a deeper, less visible, anti-Black racism. In other words, the root of anti-Blackness isn't political, and racism isn't fundamentally "systemic," because anti-Blackness is first and foremost entirely unconscious and libidinal – that is, it resides in a form of collective desire before finding expression in political and social institutions.

In contemporary radical discourse, neglected categories, such as race, are often politicized in order to be taken seriously. Reappropriating categories shaped by a long history of violence and discrimination in the name of social justice is a very common tool in the rhetorical arsenal of contemporary movements and intellectuals. Writers such as the British Black scholar Kehinde Andrews or the African American philosopher Tommie Shelby, for example, defend an essentially political conception of Blackness which, according to them, stands in stark contrast to any cultural interpretation of the Black condition. For them, being Black doesn't primarily mean laying claim to an African lineage, a pre-colonial spiritual kinship, or a non-European metaphysics. Blackness means forging political subjects who deploy their agency to respond, out of necessity, to anti-Black racism. In other words, it is "a conception of solidarity based strictly on the shared experience of racial oppression and a joint commitment to resist it."[22] It is a matter of acknowledging the diversity of cultural expressions of Blackness in regard to gender, nationality, sexuality, etc., in order to avoid enshrining a single cultural standard of the Black condition.

Framing Blackness as an engaged struggle against negative social experiences is seen as combating cultural intolerance, even biologism. As Andrews writes, "Blackness is not about the colour, or even the blood, but is founded on what they both represent. We *choose* to see the connection to Africa and the Diaspora as important."[23] This emphasis on choice that underlies Blackness underestimates the pervasiveness of anti-Blackness that has shaped both Black cultural forms and anti-racist political movements. Ultimately, both cultural and political approaches see anti-Blackness as a phenomenon of contingency rather than an essential fact that fundamentally defines Black life. In other words, proponents of a political Blackness acknowledge that the Black condition is the product of anti-Black hatred. But, at the same time, they claim that politicizing this situation provides a way out of this purely negative definition of Black people, or at least a way of changing its value. This falls in line with the well-known process of reclaiming, and therefore reversing, stigmas: of course, being Black has historically been defined as an abjection, but Black subjects themselves are free to lay claim to this category and change its meaning through their political engagement.

Afropessimists object to this political interpretation of Blackness because, as Jared Sexton has put it, "black social life does not negate black social death by inhabiting it and vitalizing it."[24] In a world that is inherently hostile to them, Black people do not possess the political power needed to reverse the stigma. They can vitalize the stigma – that is, experience it and inhabit it differently – but anti-Blackness will still have the last word. Anti-Blackness makes it impossible for Black people to escape their Blackness, while, at the same time, stifling any attempt to reverse the meaning of Blackness. For Afropessimists, Blackness isn't subjective, but objective in absolute terms. It is rooted in a social death that contaminates politics as well as culture. Reversing stigmas is primarily driven by the stigma itself. It guides and commands any transformative effort. Afropessimism invites Black people to inhabit their Blackness for what it is, without lending too much credence to the supposed consolation offered by a political conception of Blackness. This isn't a complacent acceptance of the Black condition, but a way of acknowledging its negativity, instead of ignoring it in bad faith. There is some comfort in the idea that Blackness results from our ability to become politically engaged, driven by our own interests or shared African values that set us apart from the rest of the world. But this overlooks the fact that this political engagement happens in a context where Black collective action is generally held to be futile and inconsequential, with African cultural expressions seen at best as merely amusing, and at worst as damning proof of Black savagery. Whether we like it or not, contempt, hate, and debasement define Blackness today above all else. Black politics and culture express only the effort to bring an end to this or to get through it.

In Wilderson's view, it is the multiform pervasiveness of Black abjection in the collective white (or, more generally, non-Black) unconscious that explains the existence of racist political systems. This is why he considers that this collective unconscious must be analyzed from the perspective of *political ontology* – that is, by studying the position of different human groups, some of which are dehumanized in relation to others. The objective of political ontology is to grasp the way in which the nature of a group's existence is perceived, imagined, and understood by other groups. The world doesn't act the same way toward Blacks and whites; the social interactions each of these positions can engender, in the same place, are wildly dissimilar. And, for Afropessimists, this difference has an ontological value. They believe the political ontology in which we are caught equates Blackness to servitude and inhumanity. To make sense of the profound contempt, hate, mistrust, fury, and desire for appropriation expressed unceasingly toward Black people, one must turn to inductive reasoning. Just as the theory of the Big Bang is a cosmological model that aims to explain and describe the origin and evolution of the universe, the theory of anti-Blackness is a libidinal model that aims to explain and describe the origin and evolution of anti-Blackness. It does this by positing the existence of a vast, self-sustaining, perpetually regenerating, anti-Black unconscious.

The Eon of Blackness

Many societies throughout history have practiced slavery. It has long been the preferred way of providing citizens or the nobility with more leisure time. By assigning thankless tasks to others, the elite can fully devote themselves to political matters, to the life of the mind, or to other affairs of prestige. History is full of examples of non-Black slavery; it also contains countless cases of Black slavers. However, Wilderson encourages us to consider the radical character of modern slavery built on the Black body. Slavery of non-Blacks has always met certain conditions: it concerned prisoners, defeated enemies, debtors. In contrast, African servitude had no conditions and didn't pose an ethical dilemma for civil societies in Europe until the emergence of Enlightenment-era abolitionism.[25] In 1550, in Valladolid, it was thus possible to debate the humanity of the Amerindians[26] while Black abjection was taken for granted.

The slave, which became synonymous with Black, stands in opposition to humanity. But Blackness wasn't always equated with servitude. Thus, there is a time, a period, a history of Black dehumanization. The way Wilderson frames the problem exposes a tension, unique to Afropessimist thought, that troubles the question of history. On the one hand, as we saw, the figure of the slave can be understood, in accordance with Agamben's model, as a transhistorical paradigm. This is to say, as the product of violence not specific to any particular period or social conditions that made it possible, but through its very structure, which can re-emerge and reproduce itself at any moment in time, without belonging to a specific period. Thus, exposure to gratuitous violence, natal alienation (the eradication of any future or past lineages), and general humiliation all define slaves through history, whether they be of African, Greek, Arab, or Chinese origin, to name but a few.[27] But on the other hand, as Jared Sexton points out, Afropessimism argues for a "long history of slavery."[28] This history recognizes the specificity of modern racial slavery and thus reveals the inadequacy of an Agamben-inspired structural analysis that lacks historical contextualization.

Wilderson thus seeks to bring together paradigmatic ontology and history: "Blacks are constituted by a violence that separates the time of the paradigm (ontological time) from time *within* the paradigm (historical time)."[29] In other words, although historical time continues its trajectory, although societies continue to change, and although we have reached the "end of history," it must be acknowledged that time passes within a set of conditions. Some of these conditions are invariable, and the principle of this invariance is Blackness. I am calling this "ontological time" *eon of Blackness.* By drawing on a term that defines both a geological era and a perception of eternity, I hope to call attention to the singularity of this period. As Sexton emphasizes, "ultimately, slavery cannot be addressed fully if it is only addressed as a matter of black experience, rather than the epochal transformation it inaugurates on a global scale."[30] The becoming-Black of slavery, the confusion from that point on between Blackness and servitude, is epoch-making since it transforms the very meaning of humanity. From that point forward, to be human – that is, free, rational, religious and with dignity – is simply the opposite of being Black.

Through the Arab and European slave trades, the incredible diversity of sub-Saharan populations was reduced to the inhuman figure of the Black slave. We are still caught in the eon of Blackness: "The social and political time of emancipation proclamations should not be confused with the ontological and epistemological time of modernity itself, in which Blackness and Slaveness are imbricated ab initio."[31] The eon of Blackness thus begins by defining Black people as inhuman and fungible beings who can be readily disposed of by non-Blacks. The definition of sub-Saharan Africa as a no man's land with an endless reserve of bodies and exploitable resources applies equally to our epoch. There is no absent or lost plenitude attached to Blackness: it is entirely contained in the experience of the slave, of the inhuman, of gratuitous violence. And it is like this because, in the eon of Blackness, Black people are held captive by the fantasies, desires, and images that others project onto them.

Afropessimists are right to point out that both left-wing activists and conservative pundits speak constantly either of a political practice in which racial difference no longer matters or of a post-racial society. Thus, they act as though the idea of a society without anti-Black hate is readily conceivable. However, it remains hard even to imagine a global order in which Africa is free and sovereign, in which Black bodies command respect, in which Black lives matter. The white condition would need to be entirely redefined for this to happen. The assumption made by those who would like to eliminate Blackness – or, more generally, the category of race – is that the standard reserved for, and maintained by, white people would finally apply to all equally. In the end, the world without anti-Blackness is in fact imagined as a world without Blacks. A fundamentally genocidal logic underlies this seemingly generous view. Few are willing to admit that the self-conception of European and global societies is dependent on anti-Blackness. This has gone on for so long that no one has the slightest idea of what another world might look like, especially since up until now we haven't even caught a glimpse of it. To bring it about would require efforts beyond our imagination, and the consequences of such a change would be unpredictable. Afropessimists refuse to see in the very real and frequent moments of solidarity and communion between people of different races, such as in political activism, the signs of a world free from Black dehumanization. This would be a cheap knock-off in place of what is really needed to transform Black lives: a radical change in the very structure of reality.

Anthropological Difference and Dehumanization

We have established that, according to Afropessimism, we inhabit an ontological time in which Blackness is synonymous with slave. It bears noting that, in this context, to be a slave is to be something other than human. In Wilderson's view, our modern notion of humanity is a product of modern slavery. There is a "symbiosis between the political ontology of Humanity and the social death of Blacks."[32] For Afropessimism, humanity only exists insofar as it is set against the condition of the slave. The political ontology of humanity takes for granted the core concepts of liberal political philosophy such as free will, deliberative reasoning, freedom of choice or even the family unit. These are all characteristics of which slaves are deprived.

The linguistic notion of difference, as articulated by the structuralism of Ferdinand de Saussure or, later, by the poststructuralism of Jacques Derrida or Judith Butler, has had a major influence on the Afropessimist theory of dehumanization. One of the fundamental principles of Saussurian linguistics is that:

> *in language [la langue] itself, there are only differ-*
> *ences.* Even more important than that is the fact that,
> although in general a difference presupposes positive
> terms between which the difference holds, in a language
> there are only differences, *and no positive terms.* ...
> In a sign, what matters more than any idea or sound
> associated with it is what other signs surround it. The
> proof of this lies in the fact that the value of a sign
> may change without affecting either meaning or sound,
> simply because some neighboring sign has undergone a
> change.[33]

In other words, according to Saussure, the linguistic sign has no inherent substance. It exists solely through difference – that is, by way of contrast with other signs. One of the most well-known applications of this theory is the notion of gender developed by Judith Butler. For Butler, gender is not defined through a fixed and substantive sexual difference, but from "the production of discrete and asymmetrical oppositions between 'feminine' and 'masculine', where these are understood as expressive attributes of 'male' and 'female.'"[34] Wilderson extends this critique of anthropological difference and presents it in even starker terms. For him, modernity is defined through the binary and hierarchical opposition between the Human and the Slave, understood as attributes expressing non-Black and Black. Our very ability to understand something like humanity depends on the existence of Black abjection, which, by way of contrast, throws into relief the dignity of non-Black humanity.[35]

Defining anti-Blackness as the dehumanizing treatment of Black people as subhumans often provokes disbelief and skepticism. We have no qualms with interracial relationships or marriages whereas forming such bonds with animals or inanimate objects is almost unanimously considered to be pathological behavior. Black people run errands, pay taxes, can serve as the head of corporations or states – all things animals or objects cannot do. But this kind of reasoning misunderstands the process of dehumanization, which isn't the simple equation between dehumanized groups and entities distinct from human beings. Dehumanization always creates a tension between the clear belonging of a group to the human species and the negation of this belonging. This was made clear by a whole North American philosophical tradition, which includes writers such as Charles Mills or the foremost specialist on the processes of dehumanization, David Livingstone Smith. A quick look at their work will bring to light what the Afropessimists mean by the non-humanity of Black people. It will also illuminate Afropessimism's singular position in debates on dehumanization.

As Mills explains, "the peculiar status of a subperson is that it is an entity which, because of phenotype, seems (from, of course, the perspective of the categorizer) human in some respects but not in others."[36] Subhumanity is thus a category imposed by groups with the authority to give this category legal standing – to make it a tangible reality. Smith takes this definition even further: "when we dehumanize people we think of them as counterfeit human beings – creatures that look like humans, but who are not endowed with a human essence."[37] Dehumanization is a *form of thinking* – a sort of "cognitive architecture"[38] – that influences our manner of *perceiving* others. Dehumanization is extremely debilitating, as it disables the senses as well as one's capacity for empirical observation. Everything that allows us to witness at first hand the humanity of the individual before us is taken to be a deceptive illusion that hides an abject or evil essence. The European Jew of the 1930s was only human in appearance. In reality, there was a sickness or parasite that took on a human form. The same can be said for the Tutsi in Rwanda in the 1990s: they were taken to be cockroaches or some form of pestilence in human form. This theory allows us to isolate the principal characteristics of dehumanization. It doesn't concern beings who were non-human at the outset, but rather beings capable of functioning on the same social level as all humans. For this reason, reasoning and a discerning spirit are needed to see behind appearances and make out the true subhuman entity.

There are two major points of divergence between this philosophical approach of dehumanization and that of the Afropessimists. To begin, for Smith, even if certain populations have historically been shown to be more vulnerable to dehumanization than others – most notably, Black people – there is nothing in principle to keep anyone from becoming a victim of dehumanization: "We are all potential dehumanizers, just as we are all potential objects of dehumanization. The problem of dehumanization is *everyone's* problem."[39] Second, Smith emphasizes that dehumanization is a mode of thought: "When people think of others as subhuman, they often treat them in cruel and degrading ways, and they often refer to them using slurs. But bad treatment and degrading slurs are effects of dehumanization rather than dehumanization itself."[40] In Smith's approach, dehumanization derives from a mode of thought, a rationalization of the other's inhumanity. It belongs to a cognitive register – that is, to one of reflection and knowledge.

A quote from Frantz Fanon's *Black Skin, White Masks* can serve to highlight the contrast between the Afropessimists and the philosophers of dehumanization. It describes an important difference between the dehumanization at play in anti-Semitism and that performed by anti-Blackness:

> Of course the Jews have been tormented – in fact, worse than tormented, they have been hunted, exterminated, and burned to death. But these are just minor episodes in the family history. The Jew is not liked as soon as he has been detected. But with me things take on a *new* face. There is no chance I won't be seen. I am overdetermined from the outside. I am a slave not to the "idea" others have of me, but to my appearance.[41]

Above all, Afropessimists believe Blackness is inextricably bound up with dehumanization. As opposed to other groups, Black people do not exist outside their own dehumanization. Even their "human form" isn't really human. According to the Afropessimists, Black people differ from Jews and other dehumanized groups in that their relationship to dehumanization is not contingent, but necessary. In other words, it's a matter of asking not under what circumstances a group arbitrarily defined as subhuman can be stripped of its humanity, but whether, in the modern context, one can even imagine conditions under which Black people *aren't* dehumanized. Afropessimism contends that Black people today are dehumanized under all circumstances. This argument is made possible by the second major difference between Afropessimism and the philosophy of dehumanization: for the former, the absence of humanity is not caused by a system of thought, but by a nexus of unconscious fantasies. As a result, as Fanon made clear, anti-Blackness is present among Black people themselves, regardless of their interactions with the white world. To approach this issue from a different angle, we might ask a rhetorical question: do we live in a world where Black skin can suggest anything but backwardness and savagery? Can Blackness spontaneously evoke elegance, civility, intelligence?

It follows then, as Fanon points out, that the problem of anti-Blackness isn't essentially an intellectual affair, but rather a matter of unconscious desire. This is the second major difference between the philosophers of dehumanization and the Afropessimists. Racist ideas and thoughts are a posteriori rationalizations of an unconscious structure that places Black people in a subhuman and abject position while also holding them to be objects of an insatiable and possessive desire. As Wilderson writes: "Black people form a mass of indistinguishable flesh in the collective unconscious, not a social formation of interests, agendas, or ideas. ... The Black is held captive in the joy and terror of the master as it whiplashes between Negrophilia ... and Negrophobia."[42] The way white fantasies govern Black life, imposing their rhythm on it through an unceasing, multi-dimensional predation, is a central theme of Afropessimism.

The Objective Value of White Fantasies

The place of Blacks in the white collective unconscious is a central concern in Afropessimist thought. Deeper than the hate or repulsion white people feel toward

Blacks is a more generalized desire, which drives the entire libidinal economy of white modernity:

> society's pleasure is subtended by anti-Black violence. … In other words, the whippings are a life force: like a song, or good sex without a procreative aim. … Unlike violence against the working class, which secures an economic order, or violence against non-Black women, which secures a patriarchal order, or violence against Native Americans, which secures a colonial order, the jouissance that constitutes the violence of anti-Blackness secures the order of life itself; sadism in service to the prolongation of life.[43]

This singular notion of an anti-Black economy of desire, which views anti-Black sadism as a pleasurable and vital form of self-affirmation, leans on the work of the Black critic David Marriott, specifically his idiosyncratic and inspired reading of Fanon. According to Marriott, on a structural level, white pleasure maintains a sadistic relationship to Black people.[44] And sadism is a constitutive factor in non-Black libidinal economies. In Freudian analysis, sadism refers to the gratification and satisfaction felt when observing the suffering of the Other. This is what defines the notion of anti-Black sadism: the suffering and humiliation of Blacks feeds the development and well-being of all other identities. More important still, anti-Black sadism is first and foremost, in and of itself, self-affirming: it expresses plenitude and fulfillment. Its primary objective is not to witness defeat or suffering among Black people. That kind of sadomasochism would require a certain level of recognition, of intersubjectivity, of a tacit awareness of alterity. Instead, anti-Black sadism is driven by the pure and simple desire to annihilate alterity. Racial slavery is but the most explicit example of this. Any relationship the master maintains with the slave is really a relationship with himself. This abstract sadism doesn't seek primarily to inflict suffering, but to appropriate and fully consume Black existence. Black people must be reduced to nothing for white people to assure themselves they are everything.

Marriott draws on Fanon's view that a perception of the world beset by racism and colonialism takes place "on the level of the imaginary."[45] Black annihilation and white plenitude are fictions designed to dress up the inevitability of human finitude. But, as Marriott writes, Black people are fully aware that this "fantasy has no 'objective value': it cannot be made *real*, unlike the racist fantasy which structures reality for both whites and blacks."[46] To say that white fantasies are not objectively true but have an *objective value* means that they impose on us their conditions as though they were real. The truth of Black existence resides in the seclusion of family homes and private conversations among friends where the authenticity and dignity of Black being is revealed. Outside of those spaces, in an anti-Black world, in regular society and everyday life, Blacks *are* criminals, beasts, sensual but immodest girls, or sexually powerful but rapist men imagined by anti-Blackness. For this is how Black people have been constructed within the modern libidinal economy.[47] This economy doesn't allow for any other representations of Black people to challenge these dehumanizing representations. Anti-Black fantasies possess an objective value insofar as they impose a definition of Black people that cannot be rationally debated or proven wrong within the system of the libidinal economy itself. This economy dictates the way Black people appear as objects of knowledge as well as objects of desire. White fantasies with objective value are above all rooted in a profound proclivity for immanence: the idealization of a world full of differences, but lacking any pronounced singularity. In short, a world where nothing resists the irrepressible urge for appropriation.

The Afropessimist concept of an anti-Black libidinal economy begins by refusing any functionalist interpretation of anti-Black racism. It must be seen as an end in itself, not as an instrument. Understanding anti-Blackness entails accepting that it doesn't seek primarily to consolidate interests, to accumulate wealth, to legitimize economic exploitation or social repression. Rather, it seeks simply to provide pleasure. Anti-Blackness isn't a necessary evil, a violence permitted because the benefits outweigh the costs. It is an affirmation of life, since one can take full pleasure in it. And pleasure is had. Whether subjected to extreme violence, such as with lynchings or public executions, or made into pornographic objects of contemplation or mass consumption, despised for their widely appreciated pop music, or admired for their ability to entertain through their athletic prowess, Black bodies and cultures offer to the non-Black unconscious an innocent promise of euphoria. Fungible, enslaved, in this paradigm, Black people are objects of consumption.

3

From the Black Man as Problem to the Study of Black Men

The question of gender is inextricably bound up with that of desire. In the work of Black feminist writers who have had an impact on Afropessimism, such as Hortense Spillers or Saidiya Hartman or those who have followed in their footsteps, the question of motherhood among slaves and its legacy in contemporary African American culture features as a central theme. A striking example of this can be found in Christina Sharpe's moving description of motherhood. In her theoretical account, she compares bringing a Black newborn into the world to crossing the Atlantic in a slave ship: "The birth canal of Black women or women who birth blackness, then, is another kind of domestic Middle Passage ... *The belly of the ship births blackness; the birth canal remains in, and as, the hold.*"[1] Inspired by this line of thinking, Zakiyyah Iman Jackson argues that "black female flesh persistently functions as the limit case of 'the human' ... This is largely explained by the fact that, historically, the delineation between species has fundamentally hinged on the question of reproduction."[2] In sum, within Black feminist thought associated with Afropessimism, the question of gender seems to concern mainly women. Any theoretical attempt to bring together queer or trans theory and contemporary reflections on Blackness must grapple with the unwieldy – and most contentious with regard to gender theory – question concerning the place of Black men and boys.[3] Here again, the work of Marriott serves as an important point of reference in this debate. Beginning with his soberly titled work, *On Black Men* (2000), he has interrogated the place that Black men and boys occupy within the collective unconscious.

"In modernity, black life has always been the name for this scary thing, repeatedly projected onto the scrim, as it were, of white hatreds and terrors,"[4] writes Marriott. But Marriott also noted that anti-Black hate and terror are directed at some groups more than others. Lynchings, which segregated America knew far too well and which frequently became wildly popular spectacles, are emblematic of violence principally targeting Black men. This violence was often provoked by sexual allegations such as rape, and if it didn't lead to lynchings, then it often involved castration as a form of punishment.[5] According to Marriott, "the act of lynching is part of a racial imaginary, a primal scene of racist culture in the southern states of America, in which black men bear the brunt of a hatred which seems, at times, to know no bounds."[6] Leaning on Fanon's notion of phobogenesis, he points out that white racial fear is specifically and intensely focused on Black men:

The black man *is* a genital, phobogenic object ... Driven by the collision or collusion between libido and stereotype, these fantasies illustrate how sexually loaded this body is, burdened by a mix of desire and revulsion, morality and imagination, libido and culture. Driven by the desire to either *whiten* (in lactification) or *blacken* (in negrophobia), these fantasies illustrate how the racialized body amplifies the racist work of culture; here, the fundamental denotation constituted by the black body is that of a naturalized sexual aggression in which the body is either violating or violated.[7]

In other words, Black men are the objects par excellence of white phobia, and sexuality is the principal vector of these fantasies. They are caricatured as insatiable rapists with Herculean strength who pose a constant threat to white women and stand as revolting and unacceptable rivals to white men. Due, perhaps, in part, to the weight and persistence of this legacy, there remains a profound gap between how African American men are perceived by society and the reality of their experience as one of the most disadvantaged demographic groups in the United States. Afropessimism has so far failed to take up this matter in its thinking.

The reception of Marriott's *On Black Men* is emblematic both of the importance of the issue of Black masculinity in contemporary African American theory and of the conflicting interpretations it gives rise to. Just seeing the title on the book's cover, confessed Zakiyyah Iman Jackson, immediately made her uneasy. But her concern quickly turned into relief once she discovered that "Marriott's work offers important contributions to queer of color theory and to black feminism."[8] The measure of relevance of a work focusing on Black men, then, has more to do with the way it supports other political and demographic groups than with its penetrating analysis of the subject at hand, a subject that provoked an initial unease that few denied. The Afropessimist critic Jared Sexton falls victim to this same view: "Jackson's generative reading of Marriott's work is a paradigm case for the potential of research on black men and masculinity to contribute usefully to the project of black feminism and queer theory."[9] It seems self-evident that, within Afropessimist thought, the discourse *of* and *about* Black men shouldn't be treated as an end in and of itself but essentially as a means to another end. Analyzing their condition serves to shed light on all other situations except theirs. Here we find the formula of an argumentative strategy described by

Tommy Curry, according to which "the only hope for Black men and boys lies in reformulating Black masculinity toward a Black feminist ethics."[10] Therein lies the key to their redemption.

At the very core of an Afropessimist thought defined by its radical critique of Black fungibility, Black masculinity appears as singularly fungible. Embracing a more uncompromising position than Jackson and Sexton, Frank Wilderson dismisses the question of genre as inherently external to Afropessimist thinking. For Wilderson, problems relating to gender difference concern individual identities, not ontological positions. This means they are secondary insofar as they have little impact on the structuring of reality: "'gender ontology' is an oxymoron marked by analytic imprecision because it collapses and confuses the social and performative with the structural and positional."[11] In other words, according to Wilderson, gender is a revocable construct, a product of shifting social relations. In contrast, Blackness – that is, belonging to the paradigm of the slave, excluded from humanity – is not in thrall to changing circumstances. Unalterable, Blackness thrusts Black people into a political ontology marked by fungibility and indignity, which remains unshakable in the face of any social transformation. It is rooted in a collective unconscious that goes much deeper than reproductive capabilities or gender-binary medical assignments. From this perspective, Black women and men suffer from the same anti-Black dehumanization and any attempt at distinguishing between the two will be fruitless.

Wilderson is interested in Marriott's work on Black men, but reads it as a generic reflection on the Black condition. In his reading, the sex of lynching victims is a matter of contingency.[12] The African American philosopher Tommy J. Curry, professor at the University of Edinburgh where he holds a Personal Chair of

Africana Philosophy and Black Male Studies, doesn't view Marriott's focus as merely coincidental or off the mark. In his eyes, Marriott understands better than anyone the central role castrations and lynchings of African men played in the construction of white masculinity.[13] He marks a departure from Afropessimism on the issue of gender without veering toward optimism. According to Curry, gender – and, more precisely, the ineradicable terror provoked by Black masculinity – is a fundamental part of the political ontology of Blackness: "The Black man, deprived not only of an identity but also a history and existence that differs from his brute negation, experiences the world as a *Man-Not*."[14] But, for Curry, it isn't merely a matter of Black men occupying a unique position in the world, one that cannot be reduced only to their racial appearance. He also insists on the *originary misandry* of anti-Blackness. In other words, the fear, disgust, and desire elicited by Black men underlie, sustain, and fuel the anti-Black sentiment in the collective unconscious. But to view Black men as a demographic group subject to violence, discrimination, and specific forms of dehumanization due not only to their racial belonging but also to their gender is met with suspicion in the intellectual context of contemporary Black Studies. However, this reality, long neglected by philosophy and the human sciences, has found ample support in the fields of psychology and the social sciences.

On the Necessity of Black Male Studies

As the African American sociologist Alford A. Young Jr. has observed, the streets in the United States are haunted by the absence of Black men, with 1.5 million of them missing from action due to premature death (900,000 individuals) and to mass incarceration (625,000). As a result, in the United States, there are 83 Black men for every 100 Black women. Overrepresented among homicide victims, suffering more cases of depression and HIV than other demographic groups, "African American men have the lowest life expectancy and highest mortality rate among men and women in all other racial or ethnic groups in the United States."[15] Add to this the high levels of discrimination they face in schooling and employment. While the majority of Black males in the United States belong to the working class, those who do benefit from upward mobility are no more protected from the effects of racial violence, as the educational psychologist William A. Smith has demonstrated in his work on Black and Hispanic students and faculty at prestigious academic institutions. Indeed, Smith has identified in his research a racial misandry specifically targeting Black men, "stereotyped as troublemakers, suspected of antisocial behaviors without requisite justification or evidence, and placed under increased surveillance by police and citizens as they move on-and-off-campus."[16] He developed the concept of *racial battle fatigue* to describe the psychological consequences of this type of discrimination. This evokes the terms used by psychoanalysts to describe what soldiers experienced after returning from the First World War, which we now identify as post-traumatic stress syndrome.[17] We might think of it as a sort of "neurosis of racial warfare."

> The accumulative stress from racial microaggressions produces racial battle fatigue. The stress of unavoidable front-line racial battles in historically White spaces leads to people of color feeling mentally, emotionally, and physically drained. The stress from racial microaggressions can become lethal when the accumulation of physiological symptoms of racial battle fatigue are untreated, unnoticed, misdiagnosed, or personally dismissed.[18]

Black men are viewed as especially illegitimate in places of power and influence such as historically white universities, and their experience is markedly different from other demographic groups whose intelligence, reflexivity, and academic competence are not systematically called into question. Curry argues that the very idea of Black men generally evokes tropes tied to "categories of violence, deviance, and sexual pathology."[19] Black Male Studies is a field of inquiry spearheaded by Curry that addresses the dearth of studies on this issue in theory in general, and especially in philosophy. Since there is an unquestioned assumption that masculinity is a vehicle of privilege across race and class lines, social philosophy and critical theory lack the tools to identify and conceptualize a Black masculine condition defined by indignity and violence.

This problem afflicting contemporary thought was diagnosed with precision by the Jamaican critic Sylvia Wynter in a 1992 text written as an open letter to her university colleagues, called *No Humans Involved*. There was an uproar when it was discovered that this is the expression that was being used in the Los Angeles legal system, under the acronym NHI, to refer to cases involving poor young Black men. Defined as fundamentally insignificant, "young Black males can be *perceived*, and *therefore behaved towards*, only as the *Lack* of the human, the Conceptual Other to being North American."[20] The murders of Black youth deserved no attention: they didn't concern humanity. According to Wynter, academics at the end of the twentieth century shared the same view, the same values, and the same biases as the LAPD and other Los Angeles bureaucrats. The unemployed and minimum-wage workers of inner cities abandoned by the white middle class who fled to the suburbs don't offer the same appeal to intellectuals as the white proletarians of yesteryear. They may be pitied at best, or feared at worst, but can't be considered as subjects in and of themselves. The Marxist impulse to tie one's fate to that of the exploited classes is long gone, as the face of the new poor doesn't invite identification among scholars. In sum, writes Wynter, "*today's intellectuals, whilst they feel and express their pity, refrain from proposing to marry their thought with this particular variety of human suffering.*"[21] This distrust of poor Black men doesn't just pose a problem in practice; it concerns the very truth of thought. Wynter draws on one of Frantz Fanon's most dialectically inspired ideas: "the fellah, the unemployed and the starving do not lay claim to truth. They do not say they represent the truth because they are the truth in their very being."[22] Wynter puts it in these terms: "The starving fellah, (or the jobless inner city N.H.I., the global New Poor or *les damnés*), Fanon pointed out, does not have to *inquire into the truth*. He *is*, they *are*, the Truth. It is we who institute this 'Truth'. We must now undo their narratively condemned status."[23]

For Wynter, the type of narratives and accounts of the world offered by the human sciences have the effect of stamping Black men with insignificance, which makes real social violence and its concomitant processes of dehumanization go all but unnoticed. On one level, this means that, as products of the violence of a given social system, the figure of the colonized and the Black unemployed reveal what this system is capable of, exposing the limits of its moral tolerance. But on a deeper level, in a more Hegelian sense, it means that "the *truth* of the independent consciousness is accordingly the servile consciousness of the bondsman":[24] the slave is the truth of the master. Society can only persist by safeguarding its most effective strategies of exclusion. To say that the truth of society resides in its most extreme forms of violence reverses the widely held perception that views those on the "margins of society" as collateral victims of the progress of modernity.

For Fanon and Wynter, social rupture is what, on the contrary, paradoxically holds society together. This is not because society fails to support the marginalized or rejects them outright, but precisely because society's tolerance of them is an act of banishment. They are excluded, or, more precisely, subjected to violence or caricature, through the unchanging social position they are assigned. Their suffering is the price they must pay for everyday life to go on as is. If society harms itself by harming Black men so as not to exclude them, then these Black men are the truth of society. The problem then isn't one of exclusion. Inclusion, or integration or assimilation, are the real issues at stake.

The principal goal of Black Male Studies as outlined by Curry in the introduction of his seminal work *The Man-Not: Race, Class, Genre and the Dilemmas of Black Manhood* is to counter what Wynter calls the damning narratives of Black men. This is done by re-exposing the latent truth of our societies, which is to say, the disposability and fungibility of Black men:

> I write this book from a twenty-first century in which Black men and boys are still being lynched in America. … I write to you from a world where an innocent Black man can be deprived of decades from his life and convicted of rape because his face came to a woman in a dream as her rapist. This is the precariousness that has come to define what Black men and boys endure as life. I write this book to give voice to the Black male coerced into silence: his experiences denied within disciplines and his realities refused by theory.[25]

This chapter will first examine how Curry adopts the analytical method of the legally minded Critical Race Theory while adapting it to an analysis of the discourse of academic philosophy. His aim is to show how anti-Black biases not only run through the history of the discipline in the slave, colonial, and segregationist eras, but also persist in our current conjuncture when the humanities are dominated by progressive and liberal thinking. Following this, we will examine how the figure of the Black man is constructed through these discourses as the "depository of negativity"[26] par excellence in the United States. In this context, feminist thought (including Black feminism) played the role of facilitator, coating anti-Black tropes from the racial history of America with an anti-patriarchal veneer. In so doing, feminist thought rendered invisible the forms of dehumanization that have historically targeted Black men.

A Genealogy of Continuity of Anti-blackness in White Humanities

A significant portion of Curry's research is devoted to analyzing from a historical and critical perspective the discourse of the humanities on race. The idea of a critical genealogy of racism in European philosophy – inspired or not by Nietzsche or Foucault – is not new in the history of modern African American scholarship. From George G. M. James and his interrogation of the erasure of the historiography of the African sources of classical Greek philosophy[27] to Cornel West and his "genealogy of modern racism,"[28] this line of inquiry has been pursued to great effect. But Curry's perspective differs from that of his predecessors due to the radicalism of his argument of continuity. For Curry, racism in general and anti-Blackness in particular structure European and North American philosophical discourse. He draws on the work of the Jamaican philosopher Charles Mills, who uncovered "the *conceptual* or *theoretical* whiteness"[29] of philosophical discourse. Mills is referring to the tendency of philosophy to exclude from its field of inquiry the negative historical experiences

and the dehumanization that are crucial for understanding African American and Caribbean experience.
Rather than taking the universality of human reason
as its point of departure, philosophy should start
with the empirical division of a modern world split
between white rational humanity and Black irrational
inhumanity, which underlies slavery.[30] The ahistoricism
of philosophy, blind to the social world it is in any case
ill equipped to address, precludes the emergence of
questions pertinent to racial minorities.

According to Mills, this intellectual attitude is thrown
into relief by the absence or rare appearance of the figure
of the Black man or the slave in modern philosophical
discourse. Curry's position doesn't quite align with this.
In his view, the Black man is indeed present, but the
discipline has conditioned us to ignore his presence.
Whether as an object of study disqualified by European
philosophers or as a creator of concepts and doctrines,
he is neglected altogether: "Black male scholars who
dare to speak about and study Black men and boys as
theory-producing subjects, beyond their dead corpses,
are despised by the academy. ... To choose to write
on Black males is to accept that you and they are in
conversation with death."[31] Modern and contemporary
philosophers, especially those in the United States, don't
shy away from racial politics according to Curry, but
rarely do they depart from a firmly rooted anti-Black
position. One can detect the influence of Derrick Bell
here, especially his argument concerning the permanence of racism. Curry sees a long and unbroken history
of racial inequality, marked by only minor shifts in
its language and strategies. It is this permanence that
remains throughout history that I'm calling a genealogy
of continuity of anti-Blackness in Curry's work.

Even a philosopher such as Josiah Royce, the subject
of an entire work by Curry, was critical of the idea
of a racial and biological predestination of Black

populations. This is why he advocated for the British colonial ideal of assimilation.[32] Does this mean his political project is more just and less swayed by anti-Blackness than those of the more outspoken supporters of Black slavery? It is this very logic which claims to discern progress in a thought system that still depends on racist assumptions that Curry calls into question. Curry also challenges our tendency to view canonical philosophers as thinkers whose "insights are intentional, but whose faults are accidental."[33] This forgiving, obsessive attitude toward every detail and development of the white humanities blinds us to other approaches within Africana philosophy, especially those that take on dehumanization directly.

The centrality of "biological" racism is emblematic of this "progressive" historiography of racism within white philosophical discourse. Biological racism is but one modality among others, and it isn't even necessarily the most virulent among them. And yet an immense amount of effort is spent proving that a given writer doesn't fall victim to the theory of "biologism," as though this alone absolved the writer of any accusations of racism. It is assumed that an anti-essentialist approach to race and a critique of biologism are all it takes to deem a theory anti-racist.[34] The debates surrounding the role of Nazism in Martin Heidegger's work offer an exaggerated display of this.[35] In their haste to distinguish between his meditations on being and the crude biological racism of Nazism, Heidegger's defenders forget that Adolf Hitler himself turned away from biological racism at the end of his life as he became aware of the limits of genetics as a science of race. In a letter dictated to his secretary Martin Bormann in February 1945, he argued that "The Jewish race is above all a community of the spirit ... Spiritual race is of a more solid and more durable kind than natural race. Wherever he goes, the Jew remains a Jew ... presenting sad proof of the superiority of the

'spirit' over the flesh."[36] Ironically, the spiritual racism
– essential or inscribed in the history of being[37] – that
Heidegger developed in his *Black Notebooks* in order to
distance himself from the vulgar and biologizing racism
of the Nazis[38] in the end aligns with the final thoughts
of the Führer. The lesson of this story, which corrobo-
rates Curry's view – a view first advanced by Fanon – is
that, contrary to a hackneyed philosophical platitude,
biological racism isn't necessarily more brutal, more
irredeemable, nor even more Hitlerian than others.
Contemporary philosophical discourse should thus be
more carefully scrutinized without taking its supposed
distance from the racist history of the discipline for
granted.

The idea that racism is a permanent feature of society
as well as of the discourse of the humanities, even when
these interrogate racism from a critical perspective, is
hard for many to accept. Curry calls attention to a series
of efforts to tame or overlook certain aspects of CRT,
which render it inoffensive and of little use to victims
of racist dehumanization. The lack of specialization on
racism speaks to this. Many scholars take up racism
as a sort of hobby interest, subjecting "race" and its
genealogy to any number of gratuitous speculations
whose broader history they ignore.[39] As a result of this
lack of specialization – that is to say, of competence –
theory loses its autonomy. The philosophical discourse
on race becomes an excuse to dust off the canonical
white authors by revisiting their work armed with new
questions, even while trusting one will encounter the
same answers. In other words, within this status quo,
"Black figures are introduced into philosophical discussions to reform the thinking of white philosophers, not
refute white thought."[40] Intellectual traditions such as
Pan-Africanism or Black nationalism are largely marginalized, and Black writers are perceived as not belonging
to any veritable tradition of thought – so much so that

their arguments can be appropriated into any critical framework, to the extent that they're made to contradict their own positions.⁴¹ W. E. B. Du Bois thus becomes a disciple of William James and American pragmatism, Fanon a student of Jean-Paul Sartre and of existentialism, and Black radical writers are footnotes to Marx's *Das Kapital*. It is believed that Black writers are being honored by bringing them into the fold of American or European philosophy and, in turn, this inclusion is held up as proof of a pluralist, progressive discipline. Within the field, theories converge in their disdain of writers who take anti-Blackness as an organizing principle of the white social order. This allows for the hegemony of an idealistic approach to racism, which defines race as a social construct, a bundle of words, ideas, and concepts. One confuses the struggle against racism – that is, against dehumanization, whose profound consequences we've outlined – with ideological critique.⁴² For Curry, as long as CRT is seen as a field of inquiry that relies on the imprecise belief that race is a "social construct," Black writers who balk at this idea will be kept at the margins, and the continuity and pervasiveness of racism will remain profoundly misunderstood.⁴³

> The discipline of philosophy insists that philosophical knowledge tends toward the good. Here the good often presents itself as some constellation of liberal political ideals or goals. Academic philosophers tend to treat traditions and figures of those traditions as providing some justification for inclusion, diversity, civil and human rights, or outright political programs, such as feminism, coalitions, and so forth. In other words, philosophy is forced to be a self-justifying appeal to liberal political ends. … As such, philosophy is never seen to be in the service of slavery, racism, or genocide but the complete opposite of those programs, since slavery, racism, and genocide emerge from the bowels of the unreasoned.⁴⁴

Curry's critique of philosophical discourse highlights
in unmistakable terms the predatory dimension of
liberal and integrationist values. There is a place for
Black speech – occupied by radicalism, activists, and
revolutionary thinkers – but this place has been entirely
delegitimized by the framework of the contemporary
humanities. Political traditions such as the Black Power
Movement and Black nationalism are dismissed today
with scorn, as they are considered to be inherently patriarchal and backward-looking.[45] Black men, seen in the
negative light cast upon them, are the designated enemy
of this dominant liberal position. Even their actual
political accomplishments are viewed with disdain. The
conditions of possibility of contemporary philosophy's
assimilationist discourse disallow any identification
with Black men and the political movements to which
they are widely believed to belong. Black masculinity
has become a metonym for everything white intellectual and political traditions strongly oppose. As it
became increasingly unpopular simply to label Black
thought as barbaric, uneducated, and hostile to the
West, liberalism crafted new discursive strategies of
anti-Blackness. This is how Black revolutionary thought
came to be considered patriarchal, chauvinist, sexist,
and racialist. Any challenge to white philosophy and its
dominance must be disqualified. But feminist thought,
including the dominant currents of Black feminism, is
not at all incompatible with this status quo.

Emergence of Black Male Studies and the Critique of Phallicism

When it comes to politics, Black men are obviously no
more inherently radical than Black women, but they
have been designated as the embodiment of everything
the liberal version of white supremacy deems appalling,

scandalous, or inhumane. This is why feminism is cast as a soteriology, offering a discourse of redemption for a Black race beleaguered by its atavisms, its backwardness, and its violent and unjust inclinations. The disciplines, methods, and ideological affiliations may vary, but a core anti-Blackness in thought remains unchanged and imperturbable, even in the progressively oriented discourses. According to Curry, a not insignificant portion of gender studies harbors the same biases against Black men as mid-century racist doctrines or today's police force. But, with the way they are articulated, these stereotypes are not fought under the banner of Black Lives Matter, but instead are labeled as progressive: "In fact, cohorts of scholars are identified as marketable precisely by the extent to which they argue Black masculinity must be avoided."[46] For Curry, philosophy has made no effort to understand Black masculinity outside of the intersectional doxa, which views it as a marginalized position, but also a privileged one (in relation to non-white women). He encourages us to "overwhelm the silence imposed on Black males through negative racial caricatures that become absolved of their moral offensiveness once they are called gender theory."[47]

Within the liberal humanities, white women have been legitimized by feminist theory as important theorists. Black feminism has done the same for Black women. Critical studies of whiteness[48] have restored the voice of white men, even if it has been earned by publicly abdicating their own whiteness, which is generally welcomed as a theoretical blank check that need not engage at all with the long history of CRT. Meanwhile, the discursive position of Black men remains uninhabitable. Some thinkers, such as the historical architects of Black nationalism (Martin Delany, Marcus Garvey) or of the Black Power Movement (Huey P. Newton, George L. Jackson) have fallen out of favor in the academy, victims of their incompatibility with the dominant liberal and feminist sensibilities. Others, elevated by their real or imagined proximity with certain prominent trends in twentieth-century European thought (psycho-analysis, phenomenology, pragmaticism, or Marxism) are praised but read strategically, and almost exclu-sively, from the angle of race.

The treatment of Fanon is a telling case in point. If one addresses gender in his work, it is either to criticize his "pervasive masculinism,"[49] or to call attention to his political analyses of the transformation of femininity in a decolonial context. His use of explicitly masculine gendered utterances or language of fraternity are all but ignored. Such is the case with the striking remarks made in the opening pages of *Black Skin, White Masks*: "Running the risk of angering my black brothers [*mes frères de couleur*], I shall say that a Black is not a man."[50] Scholars either reduce this to a masculine bias or interpret it in abstract and humanist terms as a reference not specifically to Black men but to all people of color. In any case, before Curry, and to a certain extent before David Marriott, it was unthinkable to read Fanon's work from the angle of dehuman-ization or the specific fetishization of Black men. Curry calls attention to this difficulty within contemporary academic discourse regarding identifying and expressing the specific interests of Black men: "While other subjects have been afforded the ability to speak individually as members of oppressed or marginalized groups, Black men are censored – told that any mention of their oppression, vulnerability, or death is patriarchal, because it inappropriately centers their experience over women's oppression writ large, and thereby not worthy of more intellectual concern or research."[51]

Black and intersectional feminist thought finds itself in a sort of double bind on this matter. On the one hand, these thinkers claim to be against universalizing the categories of masculinity and femininity and to account for the specific position of non-white men, but, on the other hand, they always collapse together the positions of Black and white men. The Black Brazilian feminist Djamila Ribeiro displays this in her work *La place de la parole noire* [*The Place of Black Speech*]: "the status of white women fluctuates, for they are women, but they are white; similarly, black men are black, but they are men."[52] Black feminist discourse claims to appreciate the irreducible singularity of each social position, but it re-establishes in every respect the universal category of masculinity that it seeks to call into question. For Curry, an argument like Ribeiro's is disproved by history, insofar as, in the regime of colonial modernity, "the Black male is defined by this distance to MAN, his nature being replaced with that of the brute and savage; he is made into horror."[53] Once the category of Black men becomes subsumed by the larger category of men (modeled after white men), it becomes harder to under-stand the history of dehumanization, not to mention the irreducible specificity of gender that has been imposed on them by centuries of slavery and colonial history.

Intersectional feminist discourse makes certain assumptions that undermine the idea, well supported by research in the social sciences, that Black men face a specific form of dehumanization. While Curry draws his examples from North American sources, most are equally applicable to francophone political and theoretical discourses. *Le combat Adama*, co-written by the activist Assa Traoré and the critic Geoffroy de Lagasnerie, is a striking case in point. Traoré methodically dissects institutional racism, showing it to be a structuring condition of Black men's lives in France. She not only takes on the pervasiveness of state violence, but also calls attention to the rate of premature death due to poor working conditions[54] and the different structural positions of Black men and Black women in regard to white supremacy.[55] Her co-author distorts and deflates her argument, which, though she is a Black woman, emphasizes the interests of the men in her community. Directly inspired by the Black feminist legal scholar Kimberlé Crenshaw, de Lagasnerie argues that: "One of the risks of this perception is that it constructs frameworks of intelligibility that render invisible the specific forms of racism and police violence that target young women."[56] This isn't borne out by the facts. In France, just as in Great Britain and the United States, those who have died by the hands of the police and those who are regularly incarcerated are, by a wide margin, men and boys of color. The wish to "make visible" at all costs abuses rarely suffered by women, rather than those they regularly endure, ultimately serves to distort reality with a series of inconsistent and misleading claims: "While violence against women in patriarchal societies is evidence of their lower status and domination under patriarchy, the greater levels of violence against racialized men in the same society are not evidence of their dehumanization, but their privilege as men."[57] To address the lack of a critical framework for studying Black men, Curry developed the concept of phallicism. This term refers to the dominant representation of Black men as insatiable rapists, as well as objects of desire and rape victims:

> Phallicism refers to the condition by which males of a subordinated racialized or ethnicized group are simultaneously imagined to be a sexual threat and predatory, and libidinally constituted as sexually desirous by the fantasies or fetishes of the dominant racial group. This concept is meant to guide a seemingly inexplicable tension if not contradiction between the description of racialized males under repressive and murderous regimes and their hyper-sexualization as objects of desire, possession, and want.[58]

Black men have been designated as the embodiment of Black difference – as incompatible with, and a scandal to, white thought and society. Feminism strategically offered Black women a way of softening their Blackness, of hiding Black abjection behind a proud femininity. In an anti-Black context where African descent is synonymous with inhumanity and savagery, feminism humanizes Black women. It introduces a space of expression beyond race and class, a space that bell hooks has called "sorority," where their condition can be seen to align with that of white women. In the process, feminism didn't combat the stigmas of anti-Blackness so much as spare Black women from the most damning markers of Blackness – mindless stupidity, brutality, infantilism – which are now seen as the hallmark of Black men alone. Ultimately, Curry argues, a key function of intersectional feminism within contemporary liberal philosophical discourse is to shift the focus of anti-Blackness so that it becomes anti-Black misandry. The feminist strategy has established that the femininity of Black women restores their humanity, making them legitimate objects of compassion, even potential allies of progressive white women and men. Phallicism, on the other hand, irrevocably equates Black masculinity with illiteracy, rapist aggression, and the logic of No Humans Involved.

The Patriarchy Redefined

One of the criticisms frequently leveled by Black feminist thought at the history of African American political radicalism is that it sought to re-imagine a Black patriarchy or that it aimed to restore a traditional – though no less fantastical – African conception of gender that depends on "regressive ideas of family and gender."[59] While these tendencies may be present on the fringes of Afrocentrist thought, neither the Black radical tradition nor Black Male Studies wants to impose some sort of Black patriarchy. On the contrary, in Curry's eyes Black men are not defined by their ability to dominate others, nor by their status as authoritarian heads of households, but rather by their vulnerability within our patriarchal society. They are not patriarchs, but victims of patriarchy. While the idea that non-white men are also harmed by the patriarchy is not new and has long been a part of African American feminist theory, Black Male Studies offers a different take on this matter.

In *Yearning*, bell hooks lays out her perspective on this issue, which, though wrong-headed, has been greatly influential. She argues that Black men feel as though they reap fewer rewards for their participation in the white patriarchy, and their frustration turns them into violent predators and rapists:

> And if one considers this case by combining a feminist analysis of race and masculinity, one sees that since male power within patriarchy is relative, men from poorer groups and men of color are not able to reap the material and social rewards for their participation in patriarchy. In fact they often suffer from blindly and passively acting out a myth of masculinity that is life-threatening. Sexist thinking blinds them to this reality.[60]

Black feminist thought frames the institutional murder of Black men as suicide. Hooks tries to give some sociological and historical weight to the supposed bestiality of Black men. But, in so doing, she ends up validating and reinforcing a whole set of beliefs regarding the inherent criminality of Black men that governs police behavior, state policy, and psychiatric practices. For hooks, the history of Black men "socialized in patriarchal culture" in North America is the story of vile individuals who are made "to make manhood synonymous with domination and the control of others, with the use of violence"[61] in order to assert their hold over Black women. This view serves to endorse the anti-Black narrative concerning Black men's propensity for rape and violence. The only difference is that she applies a constructivist approach to understand the causes of this violence and displays a benevolent concern for the subjects. Still, she doesn't contradict the anti-Black narrative; she broadens its theoretical reach.

Black Male Studies stands in stark contrast to this. One of its goals is entirely to redefine the very notion of the patriarchy. In this respect, Black Male Studies follows closely in the footsteps of Frantz Fanon, who defined what he called the patriarchal European family in the following terms:

> In Europe the family represents the way the world reveals itself to the child. The family structure and the national structure are closely connected. Militarization and a centralized authority in a country automatically result in a resurgence of the father's authority. In Europe and in every so-called civilized or civilizing country the family represents a piece of the nation.[62]

In other words, the patriarchy has little to do with the desire for domination or with virile aggression. Nor can it be limited to a collective organization of masculine privilege. Instead, it is tied to the imperialist state, the white European family, and the relationship between these two entities. The family is governed the same way a nation is governed. The family should serve the State and produce docile subjects that conform to its demands. Underlying this family are racial stereotypes and fantasies that impact national belonging, health outcomes, and mortality in an imperial context. In other words, belonging to the dominant social group is a necessary condition of the patriarchy. There is no patriarchy without the sovereign power the Nation-State bestows on the white patriarchy. And in this imperialist and colonial context, white women are not slaves to men, but rather second in command as they rule over the inferior races side by side with their white male counterparts. As Curry points out, white women were instrumental to the colonial enterprise: "The vulnerability the white woman exhibited toward the racialized (male) *other* established her moral superiority to the savage brute who would threaten her piety."[63] In other words, they personified and embodied the European *mission civilisatrice*. The first women's rights activists in North America who demanded to be recognized for the role they played in shaping civilization did not, then, put up a fight against the patriarchy. Instead, they helped perfect it.

Further developing Fanon's insights, Curry describes the patriarchy thus as "a system of white male domination that uses racism, capitalism, militarism, and sexual violence to subjugate the multiple others created as degradations of Western man."[64] Such a system is the product of a colonial and imperial modernity built on slavery. Not only are Black men excluded from the benefits of the patriarchy, as hooks argued, but this patriarchy explicitly depends on their exclusion. It was designed to exploit them, lynch them, control them, incarcerate as many of them as possible, and drive them toward death. Non-white men, Curry emphasizes, "have been shown to experience the most extreme forms of violence and discrimination in patriarchal societies throughout the world."[65] And yet Black men are portrayed as inescapably savage, and any effort they make to break free from the anti-Black patriarchy is caricatured as a yearning to appropriate the power of white men. There is seemingly no way out of the patriarchy for Black men except through the patriarchy itself.

The notion of "toxic masculinity" makes similar assumptions, often citing the sexual aggression of non-white men as a case in point. This originated in the progressive and liberal discourse on gender, which we're taught to accept as the lone credible antidote to white supremacy. The paradigms adopted by racists and feminists only differ in the causes they point to: natural and cultural for the former, sociological for the latter. Indeed, for feminists, due to their lack of access to the benefits of masculinity, Black men often direct their frustration at the women of their community. Unable to meet the social expectations of masculinity (in terms of income or job security, for example), Black men, they argue, resort to phallocratic aggression in order to compensate for the benefits of the patriarchy that remain out of reach. This narrative, which caricatures non-white men, is tailor-made for Black and decolonial feminists: it allows them to find common ground with white political traditions that are essential to the "sisterhood" project. One can draw on the most racist tropes while remaining morally pure through an exaggerated expression of compassion for these "toxic" but socially impoverished males. However, the rhetorical convenience and formal elegance of a discourse say nothing of the empirical reality. Countering this narrative that dehumanizes Black men, Black Male Studies challenges the very notion of Black "toxic masculinity." More precisely, this new discipline calls into question the accepted view that Black men are overly violent toward Black women, such as in cases of domestic abuse:

> In sharp contrast to the white community, in Black communities IPV [intimate partner violence] was found to be exceptionally defined by bidirectionality. … In Black communities, there is no fixed perpe-trator or victim: Black men and women can be both

simultaneously and often are. In this sense, bidirectionality signals that Black IPV is rooted in mutual
victimization and violence; these patterns consequently
socialize men, women, and children into cycles of
mutual conflict in which perpetrators cannot be clearly
marked.[66]

Male domestic violence within Black communities
shouldn't be ignored or denied. But the fact that it occurs
on a comparable level to female domestic violence must
be taken into account. This means that the cause of
this aggression isn't to be found in the frustrations
or complexes tied to masculinity, but rather in the
specific history of Black communities in North America
where, for generations, women, men, and children were
socialized in a context of violence, poverty, humiliation, and indignity. There is no reason to believe
women could miraculously emerge from these dire
conditions unharmed while Black men remain irrevocably damaged. In reality, as Curry shows by drawing
on the work of the sociologist Noel A. Cazenave,
"middle-class Black men, those thought to embrace
the ideals of hegemonic masculinity most readily, have
more progressive gender attitudes than white men."[67]
In direct contrast to the widely embraced explanation
for "toxic masculinity," it bears asking whether the
experience of oppression suffered by Black men, rather
than transforming them into vengeful, frustrated, and
violent beasts, has actually made them more empathetic,
understanding, and compassionate toward other people
who have suffered oppression, especially due to their
gender or sexual orientation.

Black Male Studies, as envisioned by Curry, reposi-
tions the concept of the patriarchy, and in so doing
reconfigures the coordinates of allies and elicits novel
political strategies. The goal of achieving a sisterhood
of women of different social and racial backgrounds

no longer seems to be a credible and progressive political strategy, but rather the symptom of a pervasive anti-Blackness where Black masculinity continues to be demonized. Despite the relative blindness of Afropessimists regarding the issues raised by Black Male Studies and a certain complaisance regarding the status quo reinforced by Black feminism, Jared Sexton has sketched some promising ideas that can pave the way for a philosophy of Blackness and gender capable of breaking free from the intersectional doxa. His notion of *reproductive justice*, for instance, addresses the incarceration and mortality rates of Black men, but also the obstetric and gynecological violence that disproportionately affects African American women.[68] This concept can be understood as "the broad capacity of black people to reproduce as a people."[69] This approach allows us to reconsider the question of the social interests of Black women through an analysis of institutions rather than interpersonal relationships. The paradigm of reproductive justice helps explain the exterminating violence against Black men on the one hand, and the reproductive coercion, the vulnerability, and the control imposed over the health and social lives of Black women, on the other hand, as part of the same problem: the American colonial practice of "population control."[70] The overlapping approaches of reproductive justice and Black Male Studies can bring to light how Black men and women are forced to confront, at varying levels, the consequences of the same genocidal or exterminatory logic that has been at the heart of American public policy throughout its history.

4

A Politics of Antagonisms

On February 23, 2020, in Brunswick, Georgia, Travis McMichael, a retired police officer, and his son Gregory, shot and killed Ahmaud Arbery, a young 25-year-old African American. On his way home, Arbery, who had studied to become an electrician, passed by a house under construction, which he decided to check out. After less than five minutes, he started again on his way when a family from the neighborhood, armed with a shotgun and a revolver, began chasing him in their 4x4 truck to apprehend him. He started running in the opposite direction, darted left, then right, looking for a way out – but there was no escape. The truck sped up to catch him and, suddenly, a fight broke out. Arbery was hit by three shotgun shells, two of them in the chest. Watching him die in pain, Travis McMichael launches a final "fucking nigger" at him. Ahmaud Arbery was unarmed and had no criminal record. His presence a mere 2 miles from his own home was all it took to thrust him into the horror of lynching.

On Saturday November 21, 2020, the music producer Michel Zecler was beaten by police officers in his recording studio in the 17th arrondissement of Paris, before being dragged into the street, where the assault continued. The police had followed him in through his own door, barging into his studio before striking him several times and insulting him, including calling him a "dirty nigger." Surveillance cameras caught the brutal and unprovoked violence on tape as did cellphone footage taken by neighbors. Immediately after, the officers lied about what took place, fabricating provocations and insults, even claiming that the suspect attempted to take their service weapon, all in order to make Mr. Zecler solely responsible for the violence he suffered. It wasn't enough to injure him and humiliate him with an onslaught of ruthless brutality (both physical and verbal). They also needed to have him tried in court – that is, to seek to destroy his economic and social existence in order to justify the outburst of racist brutality he had just endured. Michel Zecler is an upper-middle-class citizen who pays his taxes – an entrepreneur in his own place of work, who was pursued in defiance of all police protocol. There was no reason whatsoever to consider him a threat. His only crime was that he was a Black man.

As a general rule, our analysis of anti-Black police violence, and more generally of racist violence, automatically considers the victim's origins as an aggravating factor. In other words, we believe the police are harsher and less forgiving with Black offenders than with white offenders. But the two cases cited above tell a story without offenders, cases where anti-Blackness was an end in itself. What these cases illustrate, and what the analyses of theorists such as Tommy Curry and Frank Wilderson show, is that what distinguishes the violence endured by Blacks from that endured by others is a difference in *nature*, not *degree*. A difference in *essence*, not intensity. By simply entering into the field of vision of armed white men, Ahmaud Arbery and Michel Zecler were hunted down, cornered, and brutalized for no rational cause.

This has led Black pessimist thought to reimagine the progressive theoretical tradition in its totality. Indeed, the gratuitousness of anti-Blackness remains outside the theoretical reach of Marxism, feminism (in all its various expressions), and post-colonialism. This isn't because these traditions have taken hardly any interest in the Black subject, but principally because the narratives they depend on push the Black subject outside the realm of critical inquiry. Every political subject is the bearer of a narrative tied to what Wilderson calls a *grammar of suffering*. This concept refers to the relation between the specific forms of violence traditionally endured by a given group, the forms of political subjectivation arising from this violence, and finally the nature of the narratives of struggle, of transformation, or of liberation that follow. The concept derives from Fanon's remark that "the black man suffers in his body quite differently from the white man" since, he explains, "the white man is not only 'the Other', but also the master, whether real or imaginary."[1] Sexton points out that Fanon's remark doesn't only call attention to the existence of "forms of suffering exclusive to the enslaved African, though this may indeed be the case. Fanon ... is identifying a way of suffering that has no analog."[2]

Wilderson's reflection primarily addresses a North American context where, as in all the Americas, three main groups structure social and political life: first there are the indigenous populations who have suffered and continue to suffer the effects of the genocide carried out by European populations; then there are the European populations – that is, the colonists who have historically defined themselves as representatives of a superior race and, therefore, as the most legitimate Americans to develop the land of the New World; finally, there are the Blacks, reduced to slavery, at once a workforce and objects of consumption for the other groups. The grammar of white suffering (such as it has been expressed historically in socialist thought), as well as an aspect of the grammar of indigenous suffering, intersect. Both are shaped by a primary experience of loss, which gives rise to narratives of restitution or restoration. These grammars of suffering have a precise narrative trajectory: a state of harmony was disrupted by a sudden event, which is then followed by a return to normalcy.[3]

Beginning with Rousseau and his famous claim in *The Social Contract* that "man is born free and he is everywhere in chains," alienation – becoming foreign to oneself – has become the central frame of social critique. Our primary state is freedom, which becomes constrained by unequal sociopolitical conditions. The goal, then, is to recover this primordial state, not necessarily in any tangible way, but by at least having the guarantee that such a state of freedom is possible. We can then believe that our alienation is a matter of contingency rather than necessity.[4] The concept of alienation implies that there was once an untroubled state, a pre-existing order that is no longer. Although it is never a question of recreating the lost order, we nevertheless turn to its supposed absence to build a promising future. White, indigenous, or post-colonial political subjects are marked by this loss, but they aren't abolished by it. On the contrary, they are driven by an urgent need to reclaim their due, or to bring about a world in which this loss is no longer possible. A world without exploitation, which no longer depends on the surplus value of labor; a world without alienation, free from the diktats of colonial culture; a world without settlement colonialism, where indigenous populations would regain sovereignty over their ancestral lands.

For Afropessimists, this narrative of a previous state of harmony, loss, and then restoration doesn't apply to the grammar of Black suffering. If I brought up Ahmaud Arbery and Michel Zecler at the start of this chapter, it was as a reminder that anti-Blackness is a matter of necessity rather than contingency. Black slavery, and

its law of *partus sequitur ventrem* (offspring follows
the womb) prevalent throughout the Americas, is
the most pronounced expression of this. In previous
centuries, across the many civilizations where slavery
was practiced, slavery was generally conceived of as
a form of punishment or a substitute for the death
penalty. Slaves were primarily criminals, debtors unable
to pay their debts, or defeated enemies captured in
war. For Europeans, Black people don't fit into any of
these categories: their Blackness and their belonging
to sub-Saharan Africa was enough to legitimize their
servitude. This is why, for Afropessimists, the Black
condition must be understood through the lens of
political ontology. This is how Aimé Césaire had interpreted pre-revolutionary Haitian society, which he
described as "more than a hierarchy, an ontology: on
top, the white man – being in the fullest sense of the
term – below, the black man, with no legal personhood,
a good; an object, which is to say, nothing."[5]

It was a French man in Canada, the governor of
La Jonquière, who expressed the ontological principle
that underlies the relationship between Europeans and
Africans in the clearest and most concise terms: "all
Black people [*tout Nègre*], regardless of their origin,
are slaves."[6] On this point, he insisted, both the French
and British can agree. These words are from a letter
he sent from Quebec to the Minister of the Navy in
France, M. de Rouillé, on July 1, 1750. In this letter,
he was justifying the fact that, when a group of
white people, native Americans, and slaves were taken
prisoner during a conflict, it was customary at the end
of negotiations to return all but the Black slaves.[7] The
status of their owner had no importance. It is only
their status – their *ontological* status – as slaves that
mattered. The implications of this ontological belief go
well beyond its stated intentions concerning conflicts of
ownership. It establishes unequivocally that all Black

people, wherever and whoever they are, are condemned to slavery. The African or the freed West Indian are both potential slaves or beings for slavery; the relative freedom of movement that they enjoy is without doubt an empirical reality, the result of chance circumstances. But, *de jure*, servitude is their logical, legitimate, and expected destiny.[8]

Those on the left usually interpret the emergence of anti-Blackness as the regrettable product of an economic imperative – namely, the reduction of Black people to slaves. A discourse of racism, according to them, sought legitimization only after this fact.[9] However, this view fails to explain why Africans were chosen as raw material in the first place. It would have been more rational for European monarchies pursuing their interests in the New World while reinforcing those at home to enslave their own "misfits" – the poor and beggars, thieves and debtors – instead of undertaking costly voyages to the coasts of West Africa. They would have held on to much more gold while purging their lands of a potentially seditious population. And yet, "in no case were Europeans brought as slaves and, apart from occasional members of an African elite on a business, diplomatic, or educational visit to Europe, Africans were never carried over as anything other than slaves."[10] While, for Europeans, slavery is viewed as an exception, the exception is the rule in Africa. It is the free elite that constitutes the exception – we might call it an anomaly – compared to the enslaved masses. The idea that white toddlers could be slaves was foreign to the nobility, who unthinkingly assigned newborn Blacks to this condition. Thus, as Wilderson, drawing on the historian David Eltis, explains:

> one of the reasons why, in the 1500s, 1600s, and 1700s, the Europeans simply didn't go to rivers in Europe where there were a lot of vagabonds and just picked up

50,000 vagabonds per year and turn them into slaves
on an industrial scale, was because the *scale* of violence
needed to carry this out was something they could not
imagine subjecting their poor to.[11]

Considered slaves regardless of their origin, Black people
stand out at first glance; their skin is an immediate
arrest warrant. This explains the singular grammar of
suffering to which they are subjected: they are not seen
as workers with unfair working conditions. Rather,
they are fungible goods that can be appropriated and
consumed.

"Since exploitation and alienation's grammar of
suffering has crowded out the grammar of suffering of
accumulation and fungibility – whipped a police action
on it – the Black can only meditate, speak about, or
act politically as a worker, as a postcolonial, or as a
gay or female subject – but not as a Black object."[12]
Wilderson describes American society as being fundamentally structured by ontological *antagonisms* that
pit three racial groups against each other: white, indigenous, and Black. These antagonisms are set apart
from other simple conflicts or contradictions because
they aren't contingent, like alienation, but necessary,
like anti-Blackness. Thus, for Black people – that is,
those born Black – there is no means of escaping the
constant threat of gratuitous violence. It will befall
a young working-class man like Ahmaud Arbery; an
upper-middle-class music producer like Michel Zecler;
an emergency medicine technician like Breonna Taylor;
entrepreneurs and families like those in Tulsa in 1921;
lawyers; academics; African or Haitian presidents. This
is why Black political ontology frames society and the
world in terms of *positions*. And the Black position "is
less a site of subjectification and more a site of desubjec-
tification – a 'species' of absolute dereliction, a hybrid
of 'person and property,' and a body that magnetizes

bullets."[13] Positions represent a collective status that dictate how one is treated, one's access to resources and opportunities, as well as the place one occupies in the collective imaginary and the libidinal economy. My goal in this chapter is to test out these concepts on a variety of contexts, both within and outside the United States, and to tease out the political consequences of the issues they illuminate.

United States: Blackness and Strategy

In terms of political orientation, two rival tendencies intersect and coexist within Afropessimist discourse. The first deliberately strays from politics, preferring a more diagnostic and descriptive approach to a more normative or prescriptive one. Anti-Black violence is so intense and so widespread that the tendency is to call on Black critical theory to come up with quick remedies and solutions to ills whose scope has yet to be fully grasped. An even starker view inherited from Saidiya Hartman sees a fundamental incompatibility between the Black condition and politics: "In effect, those subjects removed from the public sphere are formally outside the space of politics."[14] But at the same time, a conception of politics can be imagined by drawing on the history of Black uprisings and revolutions themselves, rather than turning to the standards of liberal democracy or labor movements. In other words, we can imagine a politics whose standards are set by Toussaint Louverture, Nat Turner, and Ruben Um Nyobe, rather than Alexander Hamilton, Napoléon Bonaparte, or Karl Marx. Hence the second tendency that inhabits Afropessimist thought alongside this general skepticism: an unwavering interest in organized politics and activism – in short, the strategic side of politics. Purged of all universalist or unifying ideals that reach beyond Black life itself, *Afropessimist politics is essentially strategic*. It isn't a matter of bringing about some kind of utopia, but of getting by with the necessity of anti-Blackness.

As I briefly laid out above, any strategy from a Black perspective has to take into account the distinction Wilderson makes between conflicts and antagonisms. Conflicts are within the realm of political activism and social philosophy: the contradiction between distinct social interests or civilizational projects. Their competing narratives collide. The oppositions between proletariats and capitalists, between feminists and masculinists, between the colonized and the colonizers, belong to this logic. The hegemonic order of the established world finds itself threatened by the plan or the realization of a new order that usually lays claim to more just, rational, or politically coherent ambitions. In other words, a *conflict* pits two possible social orders against each other; the existing order, and another order fighting to take its place.

An *antagonism*, on the contrary, is a matter of political ontology rather than of social relations or identity positions. According to Wilderson, the antagonism that structures the modern world (that is, what I am calling "the eon of Blackness"), pitting dehumanized slaves against their masters – which is to say, against humans – hinges on three fundamental beliefs. First, Blackness isn't an identity, but an inescapable, ontological position tied to birth.[15] There is no transition or transformation out of Blackness. Second, there is no ready narrative that posits the end of anti-Blackness in the world, no post-anti-Black world order driven by the same logic or rationality underlying a Marxist or feminist vision of the future. Anti-Blackness isn't the end point of some form of historical progress at work in our current moment. In other words, there is no indication whatsoever that the anti-Blackness pervading every continent could retreat before some kind of opposition, some kind of social or political *conflict*. We are dealing rather with an antagonism, since the subaltern and inhuman position of Black people is what supports the very foundation of the global collective unconscious. Without it, humanity falls apart. Which brings us to the third belief: as a form of pure negativity, Blackness demands that states and civil society be abolished rather than reformed.

Afropessimists often sum up their political objectives by citing Fanon's *Black Skin, White Masks*, a citation which in fact comes from Aimé Césaire's *Return to My Native Land*: "the only thing worth the effort of starting" is nothing other than "the end of the world."[16] Besides the uncertainty and confusion it provokes, calling for the *end of the world* seems at first glance fundamentally opposed to any strategic ambitions. According to the French Marxist philosopher Isabelle Garo, "strategy in the full sense of the term is a theoretical-practical reflection, always situated in concrete, singular circumstances, and which strives to define the goals of political action in relation to the means of political action."[17] In other words, strategic thought defines its political goals and actions in relation to a set of existing conditions, adjusting them and adapting them as these conditions themselves change. Afropessimism is often criticized for its lack of clarity regarding its political goals.

But is the apocalyptic, end-of-the-world rhetoric really more hollow and less realistic than the groundless triumphalism that pervades contemporary Black critical theory? For example, why should anyone unthinkingly accept the vision of the influential Black feminist critic Patricia Hill Collins when she asks us to view "the world as a dynamic place where the goal is not merely to survive or to fit in or to cope; rather, it becomes a place where we feel ownership and accountability" – an ethics, characteristic of North American liberal politics, according to which "there is always a choice, and power to act, no matter how bleak the situation may appear to be."[18] Let's try to imagine, then, the set of choices arrayed before the lynching victim with a noose around his neck surrounded by a roaring crowd. Liberal optimism toward the dynamic possibilities of this world is perhaps nothing other than the flipside of the despair felt by the challenge of bringing about a new one. This optimistic spirit is expressed by the philosopher Cornel West when he preaches that "America – this monument to the genius of ordinary men and women, this place where hope becomes capacity, this long halting turn of the no into the yes – needs citizens who love it enough to reimagine and remake it."[19] Is this apology for the United States, which frames it as a land of perpetual progress, really based on a careful and sensitive reading of our current conjuncture, or is it a statement of principle designed to reassure the reader or the potential white political ally regarding the inoffensive nature of Black politics?

Faith in America, individual responsibility, and promise for all – the pillars of contemporary Black liberal political thought – are less justifiable than Afropessimistic hostility toward the political legacy of liberalism. Skepticism toward this kind of progressivism is fueled by the persistence of racism many Black people face on a daily basis. For Afropessimism and for Black Male Studies, there is reason to despair – objective reasons, in fact, that are rooted in the history of Africa and the diaspora. Their emphasis on despair is not, then, a moral miscalculation or conceptual misstep. As Tommy Curry puts it in unsparing terms: "Because Black maleness is pessimism – literally the foundation of the dissatisfaction and hopelessness in the order of anti-Blackness sustained by society and thought – the study of his actual being is shunned, erased for the convenience of maintaining a political narrative of racial advancement and equality able to be explained by less material and more intersectional/poststructural theoretical accounts."[20] The seemingly nihilistic goals of Afropessimism are no less realistic or compelling than the faith placed in the promise of American democracy by left-leaning Black thinkers.

Like the bright future promised by Collins or West, the Afropessimist "end of the world" is a floating signifier ready to be taken up, defined, and mobilized by strategic thought and militant action in response to our current conjuncture. But there is no denying that it carries with it other connotations: it brims over with hostility and unleashes a menacing and merciless critique of almost every facet of today's life. Historically, this has always been the beating heart of Black radicalism, from the first uprisings against slavery to protests in the twenty-first century: "'Mad at the world' is Black folks at their best."[21] A Black nation in North America, the "fire burn Babylon" of Rastafari Jamaicans, the revolutionary unity of the African continent, and the return of descendants of slaves are but some manifestations of the "end-of-the-world" Black political strategy in the past two centuries. More than any other contemporary intellectual tradition, Afropessimism and Black Male Studies take back up the notion of African political autonomy that was at the heart of the Black radical tradition, but which was largely abandoned in favor of the current consensus around radical liberalism in academic circles and professional politics. This dogma readily assumes that Black salvation depends on overcoming Blackness, either through integration or by being subsumed within a broader coalition.

To oppose this consensus is to oppose the political strategy informed by the concept of hegemony, which has been integral to radical thinking in the last century, especially since the 1980s. The political strategy of Blackness can't be a hegemonic strategy for it is first and foremost a strategy of separation. First developed in the context of fascism by the intellectual and Italian communist leader Antonio Gramsci, the modern concept of hegemony has become one of the central tenets of leftist social philosophy, particularly in Europe. In Gramsci, the notion of hegemony explains how a given political position comes to dominate all others, how the interests of diverse social groups come together and assert themselves as universally accepted and morally driven principles within a broader culture. Mediating between social groups, mediating between theory and practice, the notion of hegemony "necessarily supposes an intellectual unity and an ethic in conformity with a conception of reality that has gone beyond common sense and has become, if only within narrow limits, a critical conception."[22] Hegemony can be understood as a dynamic and reflexive strategy to seize power for a majority by building consensus across a diversity of groups.

Two related but separate conjunctures help to explain why this concept gained traction in Western Europe (especially Great Britain) at the end of the twentieth century. The first was the weakening, then the collapse, of self-described Socialist regimes – namely, the "Eastern Bloc." The second concerns the proliferation of new struggles – for minority rights, ecological awareness, etc. – in the post-May '68 environment. In the wake of the collapse of the Soviet Union and grieving the loss of a working class framed by Marx as the subject of history, the new purpose of the left became to assemble a broad coalition around many different struggles. As the principal authors of this strategy – Ernesto Laclau and Chantal Mouffe – describe it, "the concept of hegemony supposes a theoretical field dominated by the category of *articulation*; and hence that the articulated elements can be separately identified."[23] They describe society as a swarm of distinct political and social identities, each with its own set of democratic "demands" to better their own condition. The role of a politics of hegemony then becomes to pose "a plurality of demands which, through their equivalential articulation, constitute a broader social subjectivity."[24] Once the proletariat, no longer representing a universal class, lost its unifying role, hegemony, understood by Laclau and Mouffe as the articulation of distinct demands and identities, came to occupy a central position in the political discourse of the contemporary left. And this articulation was defined as "any practice establishing a relation among elements such that their identity is modified as a result of the articulatory practice."[25] How do Black people fit in this hegemonic strategy? The idea that the Black condition would find expression in this coalition, while the world remains governed by the anti-Blackness described by Afropessimism and Black Male Studies, strains reason.[26] "Civil society," Wilderson writes, "is the terrain where hegemony is produced, contested, mapped. And the invitation to participate in hegemony's gestures of influence, leadership, and consent is not extended to the black subject. We live in the world, but exist outside of civil society."[27]

Drawing on Laclau's reflections,[28] the critic Stuart Hall takes a different approach to that of Wilderson. His interpretation of the Black condition falls in line with a politics of hegemony. According to him, "Hegemony is not the disappearance or destruction of difference. It is the construction of a collective will through difference."[29] However, the desire to respect differences implies, in fact, a revocation of any pronounced difference that stands in the way of a more generalized articulation. As a result, Hall recognizes that, in order to be compatible with the hegemonic strategy, Black people can't foreground Blackness but must consider themselves as cultural minorities among others: West Indians, sub-Saharians from different countries, etc. This dodges the ontological question stemming from the maxim "all Black people, regardless of their origin, are slaves," and replaces it with questions of identity tied to national or folkloric belonging. It is not surprising that Hall makes his point by identifying artists who

> contest the notion of blackness because they want to make a differentiation between people who are black from one kind of society and people who are black from another. ... Some of the most important work in film and photography and nearly all the most important work in popular music is coming from this new recognition of identity that I am speaking about.[30]

But this ignores that what may be meaningful in the realm of art and culture may be ineffective in political organizing. The mass appeal of Black Lives Matter has demonstrated that, in North America and Western Europe at the start of this century, Blackness as a dehumanized position subject to gratuitous violence has done more to bring together and mobilize people of African descent than all the fragmented cultural identities Hall champions.[31]

In stark contrast to this, Wilderson advocates for a "framework that allows us to substitute a culture of politics for a politics of culture"[32] – that is, to see political ontology as that which fundamentally defines Blackness, where a particular Black culture has only marginal significance compared to one's exposure to gratuitous violence. Blackness remains unchanged within a politics of hegemony. This is why Hall strives to simply erase it from the equation in favor of a multiplicity of cultural identities, which are more malleable and from which are absent the *antagonisms* that pervade the Black position. As Wilderson writes, "it is impossible to divorce Blackness from captivity, mutilation, and the pleasure of non-Blacks."[33] Black people aren't articulated within a politics of hegemony; rather, they are held captive by it. They are consumed, absorbed, cannibalized by it. The role of a politics of hegemony embraced by the white left is to turn the desire of Black people against themselves – that is, toward temporary and imperfect forms of relief from their condition. This failure to engage in a more radical and head-on fight against anti-Blackness only reinforces the latter.

Arguing that Black experience is a matter of culture and identity rather than political ontology is strategic on the part of theorists of hegemony. Hall's erasure of Blackness aimed to *open a space* for Black participation within a politics of hegemony. But for the intellectuals who have since radicalized Hall's position, Blackness is erased in order to *force* Black participation in this political strategy. In this respect, many current critiques of Afropessimism are simply rehashing old attacks that disqualified "Black self-activity" as an "oxymoron."[34] This trend is particularly evident in the work *Mistaken Identity* by the Pakistani-born American Asad Haider. This collection of anti-Black idiocies shamelessly reduces Blackness to a subjective issue, and race more generally to an ideology. But its most egregious misreading of our contemporary moment concerns the emergence of the Black middle class in the US. According to Haider, if Black nationalism had successfully become a revolutionary doctrine, it would have slowly grown politically irrelevant by turning its focus away from class struggle, thereby becoming a privileged tool used to enforce the status quo: "the lingering ideologies of racial unity left over from the Black Power movement rationalized the top-down control of the black elite, which worked to obscure class differences as it secured its own entry into the mainstream."[35]

There are two competing interpretations of the ethical or existential conditions of the relatively recent emergence of a Black political elite in the United States. The first is expressed by Haider and posits that there is a continuity, however tenuous and distorted, between various facets of Black radicalism of the last century and today's Black liberalism. The second, found for example in the work of Keeanga-Yamahtta Taylor,[36] but also in Tommy Curry's or Frank Wilderson's work, argues that this same elite is the result of a symbolic and experiential rupture between the Black middle class and the Black working class. Indeed, the most emblematic figures of today's Black elite belie Haider's interpretation – as seen in the rise of Barack Obama, who sought wider acceptance in his first campaign by disassociating himself publicly from the anti-imperialist rhetoric of his former friend and pastor, the Black liberation theologian Jeremiah Wright; or of Vice President Kamala Harris, who built her career by projecting an image of an inflexible and merciless prosecutor of Black men. In other words, it is the support of anti-Black white people that determines Black success, not Black solidarity across class lines.

As Tommy Curry has explained, the Black elite isn't the product of the collapse of Black nationalism, but rather of post-racial utopias of which Haider's thinking offers a leftist variant. The dominant identity politics isn't issuing a call for racial unity. On the contrary, it performs and accentuates the symbolic distance between respectable Black people and thugs from the ghetto, with the former ready to kill or imprison en masse the latter to prove their loyalty to the status quo: "Hating them solidifies the class position and indicates the class aspirations of other Blacks."[37] In this world, while it can pay to feign racial solidarity, as the scandals surrounding Patrisse Cullors, the co-founder of Black Lives Matter who used the movement to amass personal wealth, show, it is the performance of hatred toward poor, phallocratic, violent Blacks that gets you to the top. The Black middle class and Black elites are not odd off-shoots of Black political autonomy, but, on the contrary, the results of this tradition's excommunication and of the renewed public hatred toward Black men and boys, who have become the living embodiments of a now excommunicated tradition of radical Black autonomy.

The irrelevance of Haider's critique of contemporary Black thought is thrown into sharp relief in his comments about Afropessimism: "The ideology of blackness in Wilderson's Afro-pessimism functions as a disavowal of the real integration of black elites into 'civil society,' now hardly a 'white' thing."[38] Haider doesn't explicitly say it, but Obama's neglect of the emergence of the Black Lives Matter movement, his propensity to lecture poor Black families rather than offer political solutions to their daily plight, not to mention Kamala Harris' career founded on violent security, all point to the same fact: reaching the ranks of the Black elite always requires a *blood pact* whose price is the killing of young Black people. Instead of measuring the degree of whiteness in civil society, we should seek to understand the reach and intensity of its anti-Blackness, independently of the skin color of those who are implementing it. But, in the face of this reality, Haider's multicolored strategy of a triumphalist hegemony proposes only to put Blacks at the service of others – *for their own good.*

Haider describes contemporary identity politics as a quest for recognition by the State, performed within the courts of law and parliamentary democracy. In this approach, it is a matter of righting a wrong and asking that one's suffering be acknowledged. This initiates the process of state recognition, which, in turn, gives legitimacy to these identities. Haider believes this is fueled by individualism. However, it isn't enough to abandon individualism, since not all political collectives merit his approval: he is particularly harsh toward those primarily concerned with Blackness. He takes exception to a group of activists who distanced themselves from a larger student protest, faulting them for their "black separatism and exceptionalism."[39] Between the Charybdis of an individualistic politics of recognition and the Scylla of a racial political autonomy that risks devolving into separatism, Haider tolerates no other political space for the Black condition than that of the multi-racial coalition. As a result, the willingness to embrace a politics of alliance with the white left becomes the sole measure of Black political potential and relevance. He expects Black activists to offer themselves up to the left or to a larger social movement, with the hope that this act of love will alone suffice to combat anti-Blackness, the condescending attitude to Black issues, and the ignorance that is eroding these organizations.[40]

Haider's attitude is symptomatic of the white left as well as non-Black minorities who expect a Black politics to serve their own political ambitions or align with their interests. Any ambitions for Black political autonomy are immediately and automatically rebuked and discredited. They are at once cast as regressive, fundamentalist, individualistic, or too identity-centric. This bad faith masks a simple reality: in North America, in terms of its political imagination, its radical spirit, and its mobilizing power, the traditional left has long fed off Black radicalism. Haider admits as much, recognizing that the Civil Rights Movement in the United States is the closest thing to European workers' movements.[41] However, throughout his analysis, he is as indulgent toward the white left, which has seen repeat failures in the United States, as he is intransigent toward the Black movement, which carried on in the face of one of the most brutal and unrelenting repressions unleashed by a liberal democracy. This is because Blacks are merely fungible goods in the eyes of this left, which not only seeks to reform an anti-Black civil society, but also expects Black people to do most of the work in the process.

Rather than try to enlist the Black community in coalition politics for which the fight against anti-Blackness is not of primary importance, Wilderson's strategy seeks to realign the Black middle class with the interests of the larger Black community. Afropessimists developed their political approach fully aware of the dangers posed by a Black middle class whose emergence depends in part on distancing itself from other African Americans:

> What we're trying to do now is to infuse an antagonistic orientation in Black people who are white-collar people in college so that their intellectual skills can be enhanced by the orientation that is felt by Black people in the ghetto. If this doesn't happen they run risk of being anointed and appointed (by the power structure) to manage the anger of Black people in the street, rather than relate to that anger.[42]

What's more, Wilderson suggests that the effectiveness of contemporary Black activism depends on its ability to have "two trains running (side by side)":[43] that of a radical reformism, and that of a more openly hostile orientation to the global anti-Black order in which we are embedded. The first may require building alliances and coalitions across racial divides. It must often embrace the centrality of class struggle, a traditional anti-racism, or intersectional feminism when a tactical opportunity to improve the living conditions of vulnerable populations and to develop a collective political consciousness presents itself. However, regardless of the opportunity, one should not lose sight of the fact that no social gain of this kind can serve as a remedy to the anti-Blackness that no other group has any interest in abolishing. For Wilderson, Black people must learn how to appropriate the spaces constructed by traditional political activism to deploy a collective discourse centered on their own condition, free from any tactical or pragmatic constraints:

> The important things we need to understand are the ways non-Black people of color can crowd out discussions of a Black grammar of suffering by insisting that the coalition needs to focus on what we all have in common. It is true that we all suffer from police aggression; that we all suffer from capitalist domination. But we should use *the space opened up by political organizing which is geared toward reformist objectives – like stopping police brutality and ending racist immigration policies – as an opportunity to explore problems for which there are no coherent solutions. Anti-Black violence is a paradigm of oppression for which there is no coherent form of redress, other than Frantz Fanon's "the end of the world."*[44]

Afropessimists are not pessimistic about Blacks, but about non-Blacks: about their ability to reform, or even curb, their own anti-Blackness. The most dangerous pessimists, those we might more accurately call Afro-fatalists, are those who hold Black political autonomy to be impossible, and consider the interracial coalition as the royal road to freedom. Often, contempt for Black politics is disguised as openness to interracial coalitions, with political scorekeeping rigged to overstate the effectiveness of the latter.[45] Historically, authentic Black pessimism, the one that bears on the non-Black world, is the social diagnosis at the origins of Black nationalism, Pan-Africanism, and most of the major movements of the diaspora. But attacks on this legacy serve to legitimize the idea that the only hope for Black politics is its erasure. Indeed, our contemporary conjuncture is grieving the loss of the global Black revolutionary politics of the mid twentieth century. Extraordinary measures on an international scale were taken to suppress these movements, from the American

COINTELPRO to the planned assassinations of heads of state, and through a wide range of attrition tactics as diverse as they were inventive.[46]

Although the organized revolutionary Black Power of today is nowhere near what it was in the 1960s and 1970s, the issues it was taking on remain as noxious and challenging as they were then. However, both then and now, attacking the enemy head on is a death wish; but today's conditions don't allow this death wish to bear within it revolutionary consequences.[47] Under these circumstances, a wiser approach is perhaps that of survival – both physically and spiritually – while waiting for the emergence of more favorable conditions. This isn't the resigned position called for by Calvin Warren, for whom "there are no solutions to the problem of antiblackness – there is only endurance."[48] The constant political reference to the "end of the world" allows for a more sober perspective on the emancipatory possibilities once offered to Black people, while maintaining "an educational project that is soundly anti-American, and soundly anti-police even if tactically, we have to work for police reforms."[49] The important thing is not to deceive oneself by confusing the prospect of relief with the promise of deliverance and progress. Anti-Black civil society will never be the site of salvation. But the resolute refusal of all reformism – given the elegant name "state removed politics" by Alain Badiou – is not accessible to the Black masses. Negotiating and striking deals with the state is what allows these Black masses to manage the genocidal threats to their very survival.[50] Yet, lacking a redemptive narrative that frames social reform as progress rather than the result of a survival strategy, the Black position itself radically threatens the status quo, precisely because there is no indication that it can extricate itself from this logic of survival other than through an unprecedented revolution:

> Whereas the positionality of the worker enables the reconfiguration of civil society, the positionality of the slave exists as a destabilizing force within civil society because civil society gains its coherence, *the very tabula raza* [*sic*] *upon which workers and industrialists struggle for hegemony*, through the violence of black erasure. From the coherence of civil society the black subject beckons with the incoherence of civil war.[51]

Driving reformist and coalitional ambitions, then, is the dream of the Black movement, which is tasked with preserving this dream so that others may draw on it. Not the reinvention of American society, but the complete dismantling of Western societies. Not a single stone shall remain; everything will be destroyed.

Canada: White First Peoples and White Blacks

Throughout the modern era, the Black question has often been entangled with the colonial question. The intensity of the slave trade cannot be explained without considering the European conquest of the Caribbean. The "divvying up of Black Africa" of 1885 precipitated the destruction of African sovereignties, a problem for which the projects of Pan-Africanism and African unity served as potential solutions. And, of course, South African apartheid was a direct consequence of settler colonialism. It is therefore with good reason that Black history is often viewed through the prism of colonialism. And this prism requires a very careful analysis of the question of land ownership. For the influential and far-right legal scholar and philosopher Carl Schmitt, the appropriation of land infuses the very essence of the concept of *nomos* – that is, the body of law in ancient Greek:

> *Nomos* is the *measure* by which the land in a particular order is divided and situated; it is also the form of

political, social, and religious order determined by this process. ... The *nomos* by which a tribe, a retinue, or a people becomes settled, i.e., by which it becomes historically situated and turns a part of the earth's surface into the force-field of a particular order, becomes visible in the appropriation of land and in the founding of a city or a colony.[52]

In sum, the appropriation of land establishes at the outset a national or colonial legal order. This emphasis on the notion of power's territorial essence is not unique to fascist thought. On the other end of the political spectrum, the revolutionary communist critic, J. Sakai, writes that "the key to understanding Amerika is to see that it was a chain of European settler colonies that expanded into a settler empire."[53] Thus he describes North America as "an orgy of land-grabbing."[54] In this context, it isn't surprising that, in the imaginary of Eurodescendant critical theory, "thought has always belonged to spaces. It emerges always in the form of nomology."[55] One can detect Schmitt's understanding of *nomos* in this nomology, which is to say, its emphasis on territory. A primordial, telluric logic is so central to Euro-American colonial existence that it conditions the very act of thought itself.[56] A progressive approach to "nomology," especially in the context of Canada, can be aligned, or at least enter into a parallel relationship, with a radical critical theory that is articulated from the perspective and ontologies of the continent's indigenous populations. The Dene nation political theorist Glen Sean Coulthard offers such an interpretation of traditional First Nations forms of existence: "Place is a way of knowing, of experiencing and relating to the world and with others; and sometimes these relational practices and forms of knowledge guide forms of resistance against other rationalizations of the world that threaten to erase or destroy our senses of place."[57]

In a country such as Canada, where indigenous people account for 5 percent of the total population – as opposed to 1.6 percent in the United States – territorial sovereignty naturally becomes the most fundamental and radical political issue, which encompasses the endless identity conflict between anglophone and francophone Canadians as well. In these political conditions, there are opposing interests with competing territorial interpretations and incompatible democratic demands. However, in spite of all these differences, a fundamental agreement underlies all these issues. According to Wilderson, settlers and indigenous peoples both possess the same "capacity for cartographic coherence."[58] This allows them to lay claim to power, to rights, to a *nomos* – whether this be in the name of the history of reason and power, or of tradition, ancestry, and cosmogonic relations. In contrast, the descendants of uprooted slaves are deprived of the capacity to make these kinds of claims of legitimacy. Factoring them into the equation upsets the very terms of the debate. But, as the Black Québécois historian David Austen has explained, leaning on Sexton and Hartman, the problem of Black dehumanization is not foreign to the history of Canada and the *Belle Province*: "Slavery in the Americas, including Quebec and English Canada, had its unavoidable 'afterlife,' to use a term introduced by Saidiya Hartman. In this afterlife, racial codes implanted in the regime of slavery operate in ways that contort our daily human encounters and distort our sense of humanity and of who is entitled to be considered fully human."[59]

But in Canada, and in a very pronounced way in Quebec, the Black question has been censored, if not totally effaced. Indeed, even in the most self-styled iconoclastic and critical thought that questions the current social order, the Black condition gets buried under more pressing territorial, linguistic, and cultural conflicts. Wilderson's theoretical framework is perhaps the best suited for interpreting the political ontology of francophone Canada. Contrasting a perspective rooted in the grammar of Black suffering with the most representative or influential positional analyses offered by a non-Black "ontologist" throws this political ontology into relief: "The ontologists are prolific because they write books and articles. But they are profound because they channel the wisdom of their people's knowledge."[60] The intellectual project of the Québécois political theorist Dalie Giroux lends itself to this reading. Indeed, she channels the knowledge of francophone Canadians. In so doing, she aims to translate their history and experience into theoretical terms, which, according to Wilderson's definition, makes her a full ontologist. She herself describes her position using the language of political ontology when she claims she is after "a thought of positioning or territoriality, a thought of time and place, beginning with one's own territorial or positional reflexivity as borne out in one's relationship to others, to history, and especially to power."[61] As already implied by her emphasis on the 'nomological,' achieved by aligning the concepts of position and territory – as well as by other means to which we will turn shortly – this political ontology is expressed in the idiom and grammar of settlement colonialism. But behind this language, and serving as its driving force, is the unspoken language of *whiteness*.

Dalie Giroux's preface to the Quebec edition of Jackie Wang's *Carceral Capitalism*, a text that explicitly draws its inspiration from Afropessimism, illustrates a tactic of avoiding the Black question in order to ensure that cultural and territorial issues remain the primary focus. Leaning on the Australian critic Aileen Moreton-Robinson, Giroux invites us to see the question of indigenous sovereignty as an integral part of the debate on racial violence. Failing to do so, she suggests, would leave us trapped in a Black/White binary.[62] If, as Wilderson maintains, Black abjection is what makes white existence pure, then this dismissal of binary thinking forecloses above all the conceptualization of whiteness. This strategy, which allows Giroux to turn away from the Black question, even though the book for which she is writing a preface is singularly devoted to it, is typical of a certain Québécois political culture. It signals a double disavowal: that of the ontological dimension of the Black condition, and that of the unmistakable belonging of "francophone Canadians" to the white race.

As David Austin points out, the Black question has been deeply repressed: "despite their enduring presence in the country, Canadian Blacks, who are scattered across the country, but have their largest populations in Toronto, Montreal, and Halifax, are consistently relegated to the category of immigrant newcomers or permanent outsiders."[63] This erasure isn't simply a problem of representation or identity, but is part of a larger disregard and brutalization of Black lives in Canada, a country that incarcerates Black people at the same disproportionate level as the United States. There are "enormous racial inequities with respect to income, housing, child welfare rates, access to quality education and healthcare and the application of drug laws."[64] What's more, according to Wilderson, the refusal of this binary or of ontology, interpreted as a limit or contradiction to autonomy, as well as the claim of a limitless transformability, are precisely the most salient symptoms of whiteness: "Whiteness's internal mutation is limitless. But what can be named, predicted, and put to death is the coherence of the ensemble as an ensemble. And the same *thing* that guarantees the ensemble's coherence is the thing that threatens its coherence with destruction: the Black."[65] This is certainly the key to understanding Giroux's refusal of the Black/White binary. Since Black abjection, the abjection of slavery, only exists to highlight white freedom and superiority, the irruption of Black politics, raising questions about humanity and dehumanization, threatens the white–indigenous consensus on the centrality of questions of sovereignty and cartographic coherence. This "binary" implies and imposes questions one would prefer to avoid.

In America, Black thought alone has the potential to radically negate white political grammar. The radical indigenous struggle is concerned with restoring a lost sovereignty. This is readily backed by many white people as it holds the promise of spiritual revitalization for them as well:

> In fact, as the most prolific ontologists of indigenous sovereignty are quick to point out, such a restoration, while bad for the United States as a settlement, would ultimately be good for its Settlers. This is why so many left-leaning and progressive Settlers take such solace in Native American customs and forms of governance – but only after they have "settled" in. The political common sense of the Settler radicalism has drawn freely on the ontological grammar of indigenous sovereignty, from Ben Franklin to antiglobalization activists and intellectuals in Seattle.[66]

White progressives are at such ease with an indigenous perspective that a number of American intellectuals of European descent are constantly developing strategies to deepen and expand it, while ensuring that the grammar of Black suffering and the binary it imposes doesn't interfere with it. The Brazilian Eduardo Viveiros de Castro was an early observer of this sort of revision of the racial contract:

> Indians need the help of white people who have made common cause with their struggle and who see in them

the supreme *example* of the unending fight between the
indigenous peoples (by which I mean all of the indigenous peoples I mentioned above: the LGBT people,
the black people, the female people) and the national
State. But we, the "other Indians," those of us who
are not Indians but who feel more *represented* by the
Indian peoples than we do by the politicians who
govern us and the police apparatus that persecutes us
up close, or by the politics of natural destruction which
all successive governments have carried out by blood
and fire in this country since time immemorial – we
also need the help and the example of the Indians, their
tactics of symbolic, legal and media guerrilla warfare
against the Nation State's Apparatus of Capture.[67]

Ironically, de Castro mentions just after this the
conscription of Brazilian Black slaves during the
Paraguayan War. And now here he is enlisting them
into the ranks of an indigenism with which they
have little in common. This is not an isolated case of
imposing a theory of "indigenization" on the grammar
of Black suffering in the field of Latin American anthropology. The Colombian Arturo Escobar, working
on what he himself calls a "political ontology"[68] of
rural Afro-Colombians, sees them principally through
their relationship with a traditional territoriality. This
interest, which can be traced directly back to the earliest
examples of European ethnology and which aligns
closely with Viveiros de Castro's approach, is defined
by its deliberate neglect of exploited Black workers
in urban centers. Black people only become worthy
of scrutiny – that is, *desirable* – when they can be
theorized as a pseudo-indigenous population, surrogate
Native Americans. In this way, the radical question of
Blackness is swept away.

What David Austin has called Black *statelessness*[69]
is a cause of deep anxiety in white political thought,
which has always considered corporal attachment to

the nation as a given of politics. Indeed, white thought is pleased to discover this attachment – expressed with deep feeling – in indigenous thought. In other words, the radical political ecology of American settlers puts on a show of rejecting the motherland and the nation, but in reality it is simply electing another motherland, an organic one that can be felt and experienced more intensely. With her emphasis on indigeneity and territoriality, as well as her neglect of the Black question, Giroux embodies this intellectual tradition. As she writes tellingly, "it is only by placing the indigenous question at the heart of political life that it will be possible to change, in Quebec, the structures of exclusion through which xenophobia, racism, and anti-immigration policies are perpetuated."[70]

Although both groups have been violently racialized and subjected by Europeans to a whole host of extreme brutalities and atrocities, indigenous and Black people do not share the same position in modern political ontology. Throughout the history of North America, there are countless examples of indigenous people being forced to marry Europeans: "civil society and its murderous juggernaut polices interracial marriages by making sure that Blacks can't marry whites, but it also encourages interracial marriages by encouraging Indians to marry whites. In the libidinal economy, American Indians are not the kind of absolute contaminant that Blacks are."[71] A common ground can be established between them, whereas Black people literally appear to be another species. The history of the genocide of indigenous peoples through assimilation and substitution continues to haunt our political moment. And it continues to find expression in shameless attacks on indigenous traditions, as illustrated in almost caricatural form by conservative leaders such as Jair Bolsonaro in Brazil or Tony Abbott in Australia. On the political left, this history expresses itself through another set of fantasies, which Dalie Giroux knows well: "The colonizer envies the powerful sense of belonging felt by the colonized, of their having a home in the world. Not only the persistence of this, but the mythology, the achievement."[72]

As Sexton explains, settler colonialism "seeks over time to eliminate the categories of colonizer and colonized through a process by which the former replaces the latter completely, usurping the claim to indigenous residence."[73] Contrary to its own claims, the radical political ecology in the US today doesn't abolish this logic, but just reverses it. The old goal of assimilating the indigenous populations has now become, in progressive and politically correct terms, a goal of assimilating *into* indigenous populations. This drives a reformist political agenda, devoid of any deep-seated hostility to the world. The main objective of this white progressive movement in North America seems to be to curry favor with indigenous voters.

To achieve this, some descendants of French settlers have even fabricated entire genealogies to feign a kind of indigenous belonging.[74] For her part, Giroux remains focused on the particular historical conditions of North Americans of French descent, a population marked by a certain linguistic subalternity and, for several centuries, subjected to the economic domination of anglophones (which is now coming to an end). In her interpretation, the colonizer/colonized division is fashioned into a hybrid figure in Québécois political discourse. This figure is at once at the mercy of anglophone Canadian power and in a privileged position in relation to the indigenous populations, with whom it maintains nevertheless a certain proximity.[75] In the 1960s, the Québécois revolutionary activist Pierre Vallières sought to politicize this particular condition by relating it to that of the descendants of slaves. To be sure, "French Canadians are not subject to this irrational racism that has done so much wrong to workers, white and black, of the United States." However, this difference doesn't carry much weight for Vallières. Calling francophones the white slaves of America, he asks: "Were they not imported, like the American blacks, to serve as cheap labor in the New World? The only difference between them is the color of their skin and the continent they came from."[76] The analogy only holds if we ignore the central experience of dehumanization that drove racial slavery, reinterpreted here as one out of many forms of exploitation and forced labor. It is precisely this analogy equating French Canadians to Black slaves that structures Québécois political thought. Like the overwhelming majority of the left today, Giroux rejects this line of thinking in Vallières. And yet her own description of her nation derives in no small measure from Vallières's thought. Indeed, she speaks of:

> a loosely knit population, intrinsically diasporic, whose existence is not only linked to the colonial enterprise, but which has neither ancestral tradition nor rights inherent to the land to which it can turn in order to derive its purpose and act collectively, which does not and will not enjoy the political aura of the European colonizer, nor the prestige of the independence movements of the nineteenth century, nor the ethical stature of the current decolonial and anti-racist organizing.[77]

What diaspora created these conditions for the Québécois? What unspeakable catastrophe did they suffer? What land and traditions were stripped from them, these fierce defenders of the French language which they fear English will take from them? Many of these defining features, such as the notions of *diaspora* and *illegitimacy*, speak to an undying mimetic fascination with the Black slave inaugurated by Vallières. However, if the passion for indigeneity is on display in broad daylight, white negritude is expressed only at

night, in secret, despite the fact that is at the core of
French Canadian political ontology. How else could
a middle-class white citizen of a G7 settler colony
confess their "feeling of cultural dispossession and
political impotence"?[78] The cultural poverty of the white
working class in America lacks this characteristic of the
Québécois. The cultural poverty of the former affects all
settlers of the deep south equally, be they anglophones
from Alabama or francophones from Louisiana. They
try to make up for it by accentuating their differences
with slaves, lynching their children, appropriating their
music, their dances, their cuisine. The specificity of the
Québécois political ontology derives from its effort to
tame and civilize the murderous impulse of this white
mimicry. But, to be more effective, it must erase the
traces of what it plunders.

A troubling illustration of this preterition of the
Black condition can be seen in Giroux's exploration of
colonial subjectivity in her work with the telling title
L'oeil du maître [*The Eye of the Master*]. Drawing
a parallel between European antiquity and modern
America, she writes: "the relationship between the
master and breeding animals is an (erotic) relationship
of pure possession, which corresponds to the legal
relationship between master of the domain, who is the
lord, and his living possessions: wives, children, servants,
serfs, animals, land and water sources."[79] Among this
list, there is an obvious, and stunning, omission: slaves,
who are not serfs.[80] The most emblematic expression of
domination, as fundamental to ancient Greece and Rome
as it was to the Americas in the modern period, and a
textbook example of erotic possession, was clearly that
of slavery. The slave, and singularly the African slave,
is an integral part of the Western imaginary of domesticity. As the anthropologist Ghassan Hage remarks,
"the exploitable black" is treated like "a domesticated
animal."[81] Recalling the words of the governor of La

Jonquière who said "all Blacks, regardless of their origin, are slaves," Black slavery and its ontology are an integral part of the history of *la Nouvelle France*. And yet the white master's gaze as he looks upon the Black body seems to be deeply repressed, even censured, by the Québécois political ontology. In their political imaginary, "Blacks, in essence, did not exist," writes David Austin.[82] French Canadians have taken their place.

In Giroux's list, women, children, workers, animals, the landscape – although all subject to domination – possess a tangible existence. They participate in being. The slave, in the master's eyes, does not. Frantz Fanon had experienced this first-hand: "the black man has no ontological resistance in the eyes of the white man."[83] By tracing the genealogy of the notion of the master's perspective, Giroux claims to go back to the "arcana of western power,"[84] but erases any indication of the inevitable binary of the plantation master and his slave. However, the slave does make an appearance near the end of her book. It is a case of the return of the repressed, a bad dream that won't go away, while Giroux, proposing a collective and emancipatory strategy, encourages us to revisit the history of Quebec, beginning with its origin. Thus she calls for a "return to the gunroom, this space under the deck of the ships where the recruits of la Nouvelle France travelled, just above the hold where people destined to slavery in the Caribbean were chained on the slave ships."[85] First of all, let's drop the euphemisms. Inside the holds of these ships there were no "people," and certainly no "destiny." There were only Black slaves, already reduced to the most implacable form of slavery even before being sold off like commodities. Believing she is drawing a loose parallel between the French and Africans, Giroux in fact exposes the gaping chasm, the unbridgeable rift, that stands between the Black slave and the human. In so doing, it becomes clear that her call for solidarity is profoundly misguided. It is here that, by way of suggestion and in spite of herself, Giroux offers one of the most accurate views of the position of French Canadians: free whites who believe they share something with Black slaves because they are stationed "just above the hold." The proximity of Black bodies kept them warm during the voyage. Then they took their skin and covered themselves in it. The Québécois political ontology is one of skinning.

Giroux's approach to politics belongs to a revisionist ecology of the lexical field of deliberative democracy. It is a matter of "overhauling the way North Americans live together collectively," or even of "sparking a heretical friendship between peoples."[86] In order to do this, one must "crack the nut that is the native Québécois, carefully scrutinizing the psychotronic effects of their double status as colonizer and colonized: this is the only chance of finally finding their place on the continent, and being able to present themselves to others."[87] The fact that the French Canadian is white in a world – and singularly in a continent – where this color has become that of the masters, that is, of humans, is forever passed over. It is no longer a question of burning down this world and everything that goes with it, including one's own condition, in the manner of the abolitionist John Brown. On the contrary, it is a question of inhabiting this world in good faith. This counterfeit "diasporic condition," this "illegitimacy" in search of a peaceful and harmonious colonial territorialization, is the opposite of the Black political ontology it mimics: that of the hold of the slave ship, above which the drama of francophone identity is being played out. "What else could we do, we who have inherited political violence but still have nothing?"[88] Giroux asks rhetorically. The argument that this violence should be turned against the colonial state and its beneficiaries lies outside the range of possibilities: in this libidinal economy, Black and indigenous peoples are henceforth the only conceivable victims of violence.

This wasn't always the case. Despite his ignorance of Québécois anti-Blackness and his tendency to be led astray by his own shaky analogies, Vallières's political program, which betrayed a genuine hostility to the order of things, was robust and authentic in its revolutionary ambitions: "For the exploited classes, separatism is, along with the destruction of capitalist structures, the means to wrest Quebec from the clutch of American imperialism. ... For the oppressed, the only response to the organized violence of imperialism and its local representatives (Anglophone or Francophone) is revolutionary violence, which is what the FLQ initiated in 1963."[89] As David Austin points out, this is a "veritable call to arms for both French Quebecers and the world's dispossessed."[90] This could have been an opportunity to think *with* Black people, to precipitate the end-of-the-world dream, rather than wanting to do *like* them, to replace them. Giroux's political ontology remains ensnared in the same ambiguous relationship with Black people as is demonstrated in Vallières. Hers is a cottage Vallières, a back-country Vallières, with no international and revolutionary aims. To borrow the felicitous words of the Slovenian philosopher Slavoj Žižek, if Vallières's politics was "the right step in the wrong direction,"[91] Giroux's is a wrong step in the wrong direction.

Beyond imitations and usurpations, a veritable politics of illegitimacy remains imaginable. Jared Sexton has pointed to the direction this might take: "Not the dialectics of loss and recovery but rather the loss of the dialectics of loss and recovery as such, a politics of no (final) recourse to foundations of any sort, a politics forged from critical resources immanent to the situation, resources from anywhere and anyone, which is to say from nowhere and no one *in particular.*"[92] Vallières's discourse combined the notion of a violent annihilation of the world of imperialism with a fantasy of peaceful territorial legitimization. Québécois progressivism today has abandoned any hostility toward imperialism while holding on to the fantasy of territorial legitimization. Blackness offers a radically different perspective on the matter – one that doesn't depend on sovereign, national, and colonial legitimacy, any more than it does on an indigenous *"grounded normativity"* defined by Glen Coulthard as "the modalities of Indigenous land-connected practices and longstanding experiential knowledge that inform and structure our ethical engagements with the world and our relationships with human and nonhuman others over time."[93] Nor does it depend on a dandy subject in a cosmopolitan world, called "afropolitanism" by Achille Mbembe and described as "an aesthetic and a particular poetic of the world,"[94] which is akin to a Black radicalism stripped of its radicality as well as its solidarity with Black culture.

In sharp contrast with all of these approaches, Blackness insists that one traverses the world while remaining a stranger to this land. Black people have no official belonging: they live scattered by a diaspora with no specifically identifiable point of origin (beyond the vast "West Africa") or, for the colonized populations, they remain, in the words of Patrice Lumumba, "exiled in their own homeland." According to Wilderson, "the word 'homeland' cannot be reconciled with 'Africa.' This is a major intervention made by Afro-pessimism."[95] The question being raised here, and which the Eurocentric intellectual traditions would rather not address, is that of Black *ontological exile.* The focus on a politics of territory and habitable space ignores that the radicalness of Black history derives from a politics of the uninhabitable: revolts, riots, and revolutions; the burning and ransacking of plantations. They are the deliberate and necessary consequence of the fact that Black existence itself has been rendered uninhabitable by slavery, anti-Blackness, dehumanization, and indignity.

France: "Vous, les Indigènes"

Though they may have been political rivals in North America, Great Britain and France worked together to develop unprecedented racial categories, modes of domination, and forms of dehumanization. These nations, like their American offspring, were built on the racial contract – that is, imperialism, white supremacy, the seizure of non-European lands and people in the name of liberal democracy.[96] However, the treatment of race in general, and Blackness in particular, by recent anti-racist movements in these two countries presents stark differences between the two. According to Stuart Hall, in the United Kingdom in the mid twentieth century, there was a moment when, politically, "the term 'black' was coined as a way of referencing the common experience of racism and marginalization in Britain and came to provide the organizing category of a new politics of resistance, among groups and communities with, in fact, very different histories, traditions and ethnic identities."[97] In this context, in the 1960s and 1970s, the signifier "black" came to encompass racial minorities beyond Afrodescendants, detaching Blackness from its historical meaning. Henceforth, it functioned as a metaphor for any potential subject facing marginalization or discrimination.

After this period, characterized by a strong identi-fication with the Black radical tradition in the United States, the 1980s for Hall is a period of the "end of the innocent notion of the essential black subject," and is characterized by "the recognition of the extraordinary diversity of subject positions, social experiences and

cultural identities which compose the category 'black';
that is, the recognition that 'black' is essentially a
politically and culturally *constructed* category, which
cannot be grounded in a set of fixed trans-cultural or
transcendental racial categories and which therefore
had no guarantees in nature."[98] In other words, it is
a matter of moving away from a Blackness based on
the lowest common cultural denominator to embrace
a diversity of traditions far greater than the term
"black" implies. However, as noted at the beginning
of this chapter, by narrowing in on culture, Hall misses
the reality of Blackness as a shared historical and
ontological condition. Moreover, looking back from
our current moment, the diagnosis he made at the end
of the twentieth century now appears shaky. Blackness
has not disappeared in the United Kingdom, but,
returning to the political legacy of Black nationalism
and radicalism, has become a force to be reckoned
with. The work of the British activist and Black Studies
professor Kehinde Andrews is emblematic of a return to
the vital source of diasporic politics, where "Blackness
is not a theoretical, literary or abstract construct. It is a
concept produced in struggle, by those facing the brutal
realities of racial oppression."[99] For Andrews, Blackness
is no longer a fungible identity available to all minorities, nor is it a set of distinct cultural expressions tied
to national identities. Instead, it is once again the real
social, existential, and political condition of the victims
of global anti-Blackness. Blackness is a dungeon; the
cultural differences Hall emphasizes are only bas-reliefs
that adorn its cold walls.

In France, the politicization of race unfolded in a
markedly different way. Due to the outsized role the
colonization of North Africa and the Algerian war of
liberation play in the French political imaginary, not
to mention the demographic significance of Maghrebi
immigrants, it is this latter group that has spearheaded the

formulation of a political ontology in France. To be sure, the most influential francophone theorizations of race on a global scale did not come from Maghrebi writers, but from Black ones, such as those in the Négritude movement, Frantz Fanon, Cheikh Anta Diop, and the whole circle that gravitated around the journal *Présence Africaine*. But if these political and intellectual efforts have left their mark on the West Indies, North America, and francophone Africa, France has its own distinct political and intellectual microclimate. To avoid going too deep into the archaeology of today's racial politics in France, it would be wise to start with the 1980s. Between October and December 1983, inspired in particular by the non-violent protests of the Civil Rights Movement in the United States, young people of North African origin from Les Minguettes, a *banlieue* in the south side of Lyon, organized a March for Equality and against Racism across France. This mobilization was a response to rampant police violence in immigrant neighborhoods at the time, to the racist attacks spurred on by far-right groups, and to racist hate crimes more broadly.[100]

According to the sociologist Abdellali Hajjat, this march "symbolized both the immense thirst for equality and the appearance of the children of Maghrebi immigrants in the French public space. ... Before the March, the figure that most typically represented immigration was an unmarried immigrant worker, without a female partner or any children, exploited at will, barely politicized, and likely to lower the wages of French workers."[101] This was in the early days of the presidency of the socialist François Mitterrand, and the movement believed its democratic demands would receive a sympathetic ear in the highest ranks of the government. But Mitterrand knew how to harness these political energies by shifting their target: instead of attacking the State, the police, and a racist society in which he was born, he channeled this anger into a reformist hope, which greatly benefitted his own symbolic capital and electoral prospects. The organization SOS Racisme, the Socialist Party's war machine for winning the minority vote, was founded the following year. At the same time, a second march, under the name "Convergence 84," strove to radicalize the political discourse, calling for a broader coalition beyond the *Beurs*[102] who were the driving force of the first march.[103] This division exemplifies a dialectic at the heart of French anti-racism between coalition and autonomy, between integration and difference.

While the founding of the Mouvement Immigration Banlieues in 1995 represents an important milestone in this history, in terms of conceptualizing and mobilizing anti-racism in France, the most significant event is certainly the founding of the Mouvement des Indigènes de la République in 2005 (three years later, it would become the Parti des Indigènes). The influence of this movement is often contested or qualified, especially by rival organizations with divergent politics. Nevertheless, this organization has managed – wittingly or otherwise – to generate subjects of great public debate and expand French political discourse to include terms it has defined and popularized. Such is the case with *indigénisme*, which in France now rarely refers to some ideal of indigenous autonomy, but more readily to the political doctrine of the Indigènes de la République. The same can be said for the term *décolonial*, whose meaning, popularized by the Parti des Indigènes de la République (PIR), is distinct from its general understanding in a Latin American context.[104] The discourse of the Indigènes de la République has set the terms for public discussions of race in France, even if this is most often expressed disapprovingly.

Although the problems of racial violence and police harassment denounced by the 1983 march did not go away in the 2000s, the new state of international relations and the consequence of these in France paved the way for a radicalization of the political discourse stemming from *Beur* anti-racism. Following the attacks of September 11 in New York, Islamophobia reached unprecedented heights among state officials, leading to ideological bluster and a beefed-up security response. The most pronounced expression of this state-backed sentiment was the 2004 Law on Secularity and Conspicuous Religious Symbols in Schools. Aligning with its American ally in its fight against Islamism, France banned the wearing of headscarves by students in primary and secondary schools, for "the 'veiled' and the 'bearded' are the main faces of the enemy."[105] This period saw Islamophobia spread in a spectacular fashion alongside imperialist military interventions, backed and championed by neoconservatives under the aegis of the "just war" theory.[106] Speaking out in 2005 under the slogan "We are the Indigènes de la République!," the movement thus launched a critique of state violence, of the geopolitical persistence of French colonialism, and of Islamophobia with its underlying position: "Colonial ideology persists and intersects with principal positions of the French political field."[107]

The politics of the Indigènes belongs to the same conjuncture that pushed Laclau and Mouffe to reconsider the politics of hegemony: the fall of the Socialist bloc and the interest in "new social movements." But these global events didn't provoke the same response everywhere. The politics of the Indigènes did not emerge *ex nihilo*: their positions align with the ideas of the Marxist philosopher Étienne Balibar, who stated in 1984 that "racism in France is in essence colonial, not in the sense of the survival of the past, but in the sense of a continuous production of current relationships."[108] Unlike that of Laclau and Mouffe, Balibar's approach – characterized by radical democratization and anti-racism – takes minority populations as both a starting point and as a strategic end in itself, not as a means or an ingredient among others in a politics of hegemony. For Balibar, the question of resisting racial violence cannot be addressed solely by constructing a progressive, hegemonic politics. His political approach calls for the left to engage in a deeper self-examination rather than a simple critique of "class essentialism," which is ill suited to the new struggles. The emergence of a politics of anti-racism, championed most visibly by the Indigènes de la République, can thus be understood as a response to a phenomenon described by Balibar in the 1980s as "the self-destruction of the left."[109] Bending to the values of the right and far-right extremists, labeling immigrants a problem to be solved, and failing to confront state racism led to this destruction.

In the face of this failure of the left, which would only worsen in the following decades,[110] the Indigènes pushed for a new political subjectivity. The notion of *indigénat*,[111] imposed by colonial regulations in Algeria and French West Africa, was reappropriated and invested with a new sociohistorical meaning. "Choosing to identify ourselves as *'indigènes de la république'* is a forceful act of resistance. It allows us to expose the reality of the Republic and to throw into relief the shared political interests of the larger community of all those who originate from colonies or former colonies."[112] Reappropriating the term *indigène* thus gave a unifying category to all the victims of state racism and drew an explicit parallel between the violence of the past and that of the present. But this alone wasn't enough:

> in a context where the "colonized from within" are a minority, where the borders between "indigènes" and "non-indigènes" are porous, where we cannot be separatists, where the war we are fighting is asymmetrical,

where it can only be a war of positions and not a war of movement, under all these conditions, then, the strategic horizon has to be conceived in terms of the construction of a ... *broad* anti-colonial coalition.[113]

France is the nation with the largest Muslim population in Europe. But it also has the largest Jewish population in Europe. This is clearly why the question of the potential political ties between these two communities has occupied such an important place in the strategic thinking of the Indigènes. Indeed, it is widely believed that enlisting the Jewish community to join forces with the Indigènes would be the key to growing a larger anti-colonial movement.

Describing the differences between European and North American contexts, Wilderson remarked that there is "a lot of unproductive guilt about the Jewish Holocaust that taints all scholarship in Germany."[114] This seems to apply beyond Germany and beyond the world of academia. What Wilderson describes here as unproductive guilt can be understood as a fundamentally *anachronistic* approach to the Jewish condition that makes us lose sight of the present reality of populations. Houria Bouteldja, who was for a long time the spokesperson for the Parti des Indigènes, was accused of anti-Semitism for having stated that French Jews had gone "from being pariahs, to being, on the one hand, *dhimmis of the Republic* to satisfy the internal needs of the nation state, and on the other, *Senegalese riflemen* to satisfy the needs of Western imperialism."[115] Such an accusation is clearly based on a misunderstanding. Many Jews in Western countries consider themselves white, with a small difference. The strategy adopted by the Indigènes de la République sought to emphasize this "small difference" in order to recall a genocidal past and to put a magnifying glass on today's anti-Semitic violence in France. In this way, Jews were encouraged to distance themselves from the French Nation-state and form alliances with the Muslim community. The aim was to reawaken a feeling of illegitimacy and insecurity, no longer toward Muslim populations, but toward the French State, which was as quick to evoke Jews to justify beefed-up security measures as it was to turn a blind eye to anti-Semites. Reviewing Bouteldja's work, Jared Sexton likens her approach to a Gramscian strategy, dwelling in particular on this quote, addressed to French Jews: "To be honest, between us, everything is still possible. I might be optimistic, but that's my own choice. We have a common destiny in the same way that we potentially have a common future."[116] For Sexton, this construction of an "us" comprising "*indigènes*" and Jews is the symptom of a "hedging radicalism."[117]

The severity of this judgment can be explained in part by the site of its utterance. In the context of the United States – provided they are not of Ethiopian, Jamaican, etc., descent – Jews are without question white.[118] Despite exaggerated depictions in the media, despite popular conspiracy theories that portray them as shadowy puppet masters, the vast majority of Jews are nonetheless a population of European extraction, with higher levels of education and longer lifespans than the average population.[119] The idea that such a group, with its innumerable contributions to American culture, science, and power, could in the near future become the almost exclusive target of new mass violence seems hardly credible – especially in a country where *any group*, including white police officers,[120] is cyclically the target of such violence. Finally, the success of assimilating Jews to the white population offers a sharp contrast with the fate of the Black masses who, to a much larger extent than any other group, are subjected to exploitation, alienation, and disproportionate violence on a daily basis.

Unproductive guilt acts as an afterimage on our retinas, where reality is clouded by the concentration camp, preventing us from seeing that the interests and cultural ambitions of whites who are Jews and those who are not tend to overlap. In France, there is no census data to provide an accurate understanding of the Jewish demographic, but the political, intellectual, and military contributions of this group, despite profound anti-Semitism in French secular society, cannot be overstated. The view of French Jews as an assimilable population, indistinguishable from other French people, is as old as the anti-Jewish narrative. This is what Fanon is referring to in *Black Skin, White Masks*:

> The Jewishness of the Jew, however, can go unnoticed. He is not integrally what he is. We can but hope and wait. His acts and behavior are the determining factor. He is a white man, and apart from some debatable features, he can pass undetected. ... Of course the Jews have been tormented – no, worse than tormented, they have been hunted, exterminated, and burned to death. But these are just minor episodes in the family history. The Jew is not liked as soon as he has been detected. But with me things take on a *new* face. There is no chance I won't be seen. I am overdetermined from the outside. I am a slave not to the "idea" others have of me, but to my appearance.[121]

This point is all the more important as Fanon's work is often cited to highlight the parallels between anti-Semitism and anti-Blackness or to signal an intrinsic solidarity between the victims of these forms of racial violence. And it's true that Fanon, recounting what one of his professors had once said, wrote these now famous words: "When you hear someone insulting the Jews, pay attention; he is talking about you," which, according to Fanon, means "the anti-Semite naturally hates Black people."[122] In the larger context of Fanon's work, it would be wrong to interpret this optimistically. All racism isn't interchangeable and the oppressed cannot freely identify with one another. For if all anti-Semitism is a form of anti-Black hatred, the reverse isn't true. Not all anti-Black hatred is anti-Semitic. For Fanon, one must grasp that Blackness is the pure element, the secret substance, of racial prejudice. It is the most total abjection, the absolute abhorrence, of which all other forms of alterity are but diluted, less intense variations. No matter how you spin it, racism *begins* with anti-Blackness.

Extending Fanon's argument, Wilderson emphasized the ontological difference between the two groups: "Jews went into Auschwitz and came out as Jews. Africans went into the ships and came out as Blacks. The former is a Human holocaust; the latter is a Human *and* a metaphysical holocaust. That is why it makes little sense to attempt analogy: the Jews have the Dead ... among them; the Dead have the Blacks among them."[123] Playing off Wilderson's remarks, we might add, tongue in cheek, that, with the end of the Second World War, the founding of the State of Israel, and the decline of anti-Semitism in the European public sphere, Jews came out of this as *whites*. This is what the historian Enzo Traverso has called the end of Jewish modernity, which impacted even the political groups with the most extreme anti-Jewish rhetoric: "The decline of traditional anti-Semitism, and the adoption of a well-wishing attitude towards Zionism, are at the heart of a mutation in the European far right movements. For the first time in history, Jews and the far right have ceased to be incompatible worlds, irreducibly opposed to one another, as they are no longer divided by anti-Semitism."[124] And what if this decline in anti-Semitism, which had previously provided a form of social coherency, was not a simple ruse of imperialism? What if this new alliance between "Israelites" and the extreme right was not a cynical ploy by an imperialist power to use the Jews for its own benefit, but rather the end of the family quarrel described by Fanon? What if the collective "we" uttered together by Jews and conservative whites was, on both sides, pronounced with utmost authenticity and heartfelt sincerity? Perhaps the assimilation of Jews into the white and European world would be seen no longer as a false pretense but as an enduring reality, best exemplified in the United States. From this perspective, Israel appears to be a settlement colony like any other born of modern colonialism. It traffics in the same old white supremacist racial contract and combines a monotheism with traditionalist pretensions and a modern racism, like a Jewish rendition of the national Christianity of apartheid-era South Africa. In spite of the feigned disbelief of the Israeli daily *Haaretz*, it is no surprise that an increasing number of South African settlers are converting to Judaism and joining the effort to colonize the West Bank.[125]

Influenced deeply by the Maghrebi culture shared by both the Muslims and the Sephardic Jews of France, the Indigènes de la République took a clear stance by viewing the gradual assimilation of Western Jews into the white world as an impossible fantasy, insisting on a statutory difference between Jews and whites. But this difference has grown empirically tenuous. All the while, another significant difference has always been glossed over, evaded, ignored: the long-standing divide between Blacks and North Africans. A minor incident reported by the news will shed some light on this. It is a trivial, and not uncommon, occurrence, but its triviality is precisely what allows us to witness the depth of the political ontology in question. On May 30, 2021, in the city of Cergy in the north-western suburbs of Paris, a young man verbally assaulted a Black deliveryman. After discovering he was being filmed by an onlooker from her apartment window, he in turn insulted her, using the n-word, calling her filthy, and telling her that, "for 800 years, we sold you like livestock, fucking whores! I am Algerian! Us Algerians sold you like livestock, like corn, fucking bastards!" No one is surprised now by the reference to slavery in these kinds of disputes between Blacks and Arabs. The young man is clearly not a historian, and in any case the issue doesn't pertain to the faithfulness to the historical record. Instead, we must ask: what are the mechanisms, the genealogy, and the libidinal economy that underlie this anti-Black recourse to North African slavery in the imaginary of this community?

In the context of French anti-racism, the Black question, especially framed this way, is harder to address than the more general Jewish question. The politics of anti-racism has always sought to minimize the former, relativizing it by narrowly focusing on the present situation and immediate context alone. The interpretation it provides isn't unconvincing, but it remains limited:

> Because they are discriminated against and oppressed as *indigènes*, a common front linking people across class, gender, community, etc., lines is launched in opposition to the indignity and denial of citizenship that they all endure. Young people from the *banlieue* stand side by side with the college-educated and career professionals, Blacks and Arabs, Muslims or sympathizers of political Islam and atheists, are all brought together in this effort.[126]

What is repeatedly overlooked in this view is the fact that the category of *slaves* always already trumps that of *indigènes*. Indeed, the category of *slaves* renders the latter hollow and ineffectual. The question, then, is whether these intersectional ambitions continue to be undermined by the legacy of a North African anti-Black hatred that has contributed to the construction of political institutions and subjectivities. That a young Maghrebi man would resort to this hatred in order to widen the gap between himself – the human – and the Black man or woman – that is, the slave – attests to its pervasiveness.

Suggesting that there is a North African anti-Blackness linked to the history of slavery is often met with disbelief and suspicion. This comes as no surprise. It is widely accepted that, in any land where Islam was the dominant practice, the determining factor in defining a population as foreign, and thus authorizing its enslavement, was never race, but religious affiliation. The absence of any scientific rationalization of racism in this cultural space is often cited as proof of this. However, Islamic law wasn't always followed to the letter – in fact, it was often systematically circumvented – when dealing with sub-Saharan populations. What's more, as already indicated, Black abjection *is not a matter of racism*. It never needed a scientific justification or a European taxonomy to assert itself. Anti-Blackness stems from an age-old *intuition* of Black inhumanity. Influenced by the colonial efforts of his counterparts north of the Mediterranean, the Moroccan ruler Ahmad al-Mansur relied on this kind of intuition at the end of the sixteenth century to legitimize his conquest of his southern neighbor, the Songhai Empire, which was also Muslim. Analyzing his correspondence with the ulema of that period, the Moroccan historian Samia Errazzouki speaks to the motivations of Ahmad: "Ahmad al-Mansūr's decision to invade the Songhai has less to do with a newfound military competence and more to do with race superseding religion as the dominant marker of otherness."[127] In 1578, the Sultan had won a triumphant battle over Portugal, which earned him his nickname of *al-Mansur* (the Victorious). In his treatment of prisoners, he broke with tradition. Rather than enslave them, he offered to sell them back to the Portuguese crown. Besides being a strategy to replenish funds – while depleting those of the enemy – for future war efforts, this decision marks a new turning point whereby Europeans are defined as enemies, but also as equals unsuited to slavery.[128]

Ahmad's military strategy against his southern neighbor won him the war.

> Following Ahmad al-Mansūr's invasion of the Songhai Empire in 1591, which brought an end to one of West Africa's most expansive and enduring empires, thousands of West African Muslims were paraded in the Sàdi's imperial capital of Marrakech. Bound in metal chains and auctioned off in markets, historical accounts depict scenes that would become all-too familiar on the other side of the Atlantic.[129]

Indeed, in Morocco during this period, beyond their role in an economy of production, Black slaves contributed to an economy of spectacle where their domination was put on display as a sign of their owners' wealth and power.

> Eunuchs, dwarves, black slaves and exotic animals: the singular and the monstrous were the privileged material of expeditions of conquest and discovery throughout the sixteenth century. Monstrous beings were associated with the prodigious, connecting the natural world with the supernatural one, as Solomon himself had done. … Such signs were to contribute to the dazzling and blinding display of power sought after by Ahmad's court at Marrakesh.[130]

Thus, the notion that North African anti-Blackness was never a form of "state racism" proves to be utterly false. Ahmad al-Mansur held anti-Blackness to be a feature of his sovereign power, a token of the brilliance and prestige of his reign in spite of the teachings of the

Qur'an and the strict proclamations of Islamic law, and in spite of the commercial and cultural traditions of his own people. As established by its supreme ruler, Blackness would soon become equated to servility and monstrosity in Moroccan society, an association that would prove to have a lasting impact. As the historian Chouki El Hamel writes: "Evidence that I present strongly suggests that in the late seventeenth century blacks were indeed exploited in Morocco: there was a clear ideological foundation for a society divided by skin color."[131] Furthering the practice initiated by Ahmad al-Mansur in the previous century, it is hence-forth the racial principle that prevails over the religious principle to organize social hierarchies.

Although such practices were condemned by the Prophet of Islam, one could easily turn to any number of Mediterranean cultural traditions, scholarly or popular, to justify them. These became integrated into various cultures through habit, to the extent that they became confused with practices of faith and "were not dislodged by the egalitarian color-blind tenets of Islam."[132] These doctrines were bolstered by Maghrebi writers such as Ibn Khaldoun, Ibn Battûta, or Léon l'Africain, who wrote disparagingly of Black populations. All the while, white travelers and intellectuals turned a blind eye to this reality, for reasons that El Hamel illuminates in his study. First of all, the European version of racial slavery was based on the law of *partus sequitur ventrem* – that is, filiation determined by the mother – and thus precluded any formal union between white men and Black women. However, in the Moroccan slave system, where filiation depended on the father, such unions existed, which misled foreigners accustomed to American-style slavery. Second, foreigners were more familiar with Moroccan cities but knew little about the country's rural culture, where slavery was more prominent. And, finally, scholars of Islamic law tended to read it from an orientalist perspective that assumed that it "could be studied apart from the economics, sociology, and politics of the Islamic peoples."[133] As a result, they tended to believe naively that the rule was scrupulously respected, confusing ideals with empirical reality and ignoring the exceptions systematically made to legitimize Black slavery in practice.

It bears repeating that anti-Blackness – the relegation of Black people to inhumanity and non-being – is a global phenomenon that takes on distinct forms of expression in each sociocultural context. It is also characterized by its permanence. As opposed to the situation of the Jews described above, which shares little objectively with that of the 1930s and 1940s, Blacks remain the object of predatory slavery in North Africa, which explains in part why they continue to be equated with livestock or corn in the popular imaginary of the North African diaspora. On November 13, 2017, CNN reported on Black slavery taking place in Syria, proving to what extent it has persisted even today. The following day, 10,000 people gathered in front of the Syrian embassy in Paris in a protest led by Black organizations. In North Africa, there is a history of state-sponsored racial slavery of Blacks, the consequences of which persist in the Maghreb in various forms – from systematic discrimination and violence against the descendants of slaves, to the large-scale policing of sub-Saharan migrants which is financed by the European Union. Throughout this history, Black people have been dehumanized, portrayed as monsters, and treated as beasts whose subjection is displayed as a sign of sovereign power. The assault in Cergy is but one example of how this libidinal economy and this imaginary – shaped by a sovereign power – are still cherished today, even in the diaspora, as markers of superiority. The assailant associates his own home country, Algeria, with Morocco's legacy of slavery to take pride in it and to take pride in himself. The humanity of the North African is affirmed and glorified by way of contrast with the slave's abhorrence, the Black woman's abjection. It is for this reason that Sexton finds Boutleldja's work, with its borrowings from Black intellectual history, ultimately lacking. For him, the analysis must be pushed further, which means shattering the unifying but unstable category of *indigènes*:

> If this revolutionary love draws fully from the encounter between Baldwin and Lorde, or the thousands of others like it in the black political cultures derived from "the world the slaves made," it would have to look beyond the broad heading of the *indigènes* and turn itself toward "those who are beneath those who are at the bottom." Specifically, toward those slaves and their disinherited descendants whose historic alliance the proletarians could not abide, whose enslavement and its afterlife precedes and belies the suffering of the postcolonial immigrant, and whose ongoing predicament subtends any and all "groups seeking plenitude," material or symbolic. Those who are not simply shorn of "noble titles" but who have lost even that wretched status as "losers." Those that will write the next chapter of this story, the seventh chapter, from below: *You, the Indigenous.*[134]

Even when subjected to the same state violence, even when they experience the accumulated effects of Islamophobia, anti-immigrant hatred, and police harassment, Arab *indigènes* still have recourse to a private reassurance that restores their humanity: Black people are like their slaves. This difference, or division, is fundamental. In every respect, it is deeper than what divides Maghrebi from Jews – which is to say, white people. And yet, throughout the history of the Indigènes de la République, Black people have been unquestioningly subsumed under the category of *indigènes*. But this assimilation is only possible if Black history is ignored. Indeed, one must systematically refuse to take seriously the core pessimism of Black radicalism to equate these disparate groups. The gap between the politics of the Indigènes and the legacy of Black radicalism is thrown into relief in Sadri Khiari's reading of the political strategy of a figure as central as Malcolm X:

> Malcolm X thus persists in minimizing the tensions that run through white society and the white political system; he also fails to account for – or inadequately accounts for – the conflicts that beset it due to Black resistance. He considers white people as irremediably racist or at least prisoners of a racial syntax that is so imposing and powerful that it thwarts collective resistance, allowing only for occasional and small-scale rebellions. ... Malcolm X may be overstating the case to persuade his listeners that the American racial system cannot simply be transformed from within and cannot change peacefully; he constantly warns them against the inclination of integrationist leaders to make use of the limits set by white liberals, or even to hand over the actual leadership of the movement to them. Having no patience for nuance, he reproaches all white liberals for being complicit in the racial system. His indictment of them seems justified when he notes that the support of white liberals is conditional, depending on the respect for the "limits" they alone are responsible for determining, but at the same time his indictment is undermined by his indifference to the internal contradictions of the white world, expressed in part by the diversity of the political positions of white liberals themselves.[135]

Khiari minimizes the social coherency that anti-Blackness gives to North America, and beyond. To note, as he does, the many divisions within white society does not lead to the automatic conclusion that some white positions would naturally align with Black interests. In contrast, Tommy Curry's genealogy of anti-Blackness convincingly argues that the tensions and divisions rightly identified by Khiari are often given a sense of continuity by anti-Blackness, which functions as their lowest common denominator. The risk in losing sight of this reality is that a temporary loosening of the white supremacist stranglehold can be confused with an advance in Black liberation. Considering racism from the perspective of the North African experience, which is always structured around the question of assimilation and proximity to Jews, one misses the fact that disagreements among white people have never been over the illegitimacy of anti-Blackness as such, but rather express competing anti-Black positions.

The empirical validity of an irremediable racism among the majority of whites depends on the power relations, the period in question, and the local context of each case. But one thing is clear: historically, Black people have never been able to count on active support from a significant portion of white society. Malcolm X understood that radical pessimism toward the white world was the only realistic strategy for his people. This strategy can shift momentarily if a credible opportunity for creating a coalition arises, but white sympathy has no structural reality and is certainly not a given, since it is not only conditional, but always short-lived and self-serving. A clear picture of the internal contradictions of the white world only emerges once the permanence of anti-Blackness is taken as its focal point, not its background. The logical conclusion of Khiari's analysis is expressed by Bouteldja. In her reading, the French revolutionary writer Jean Genet "intimates that behind Malcolm X's radical resistance is his own salvation"[136] – that is, his salvation as a white person.

French anti-racist discourse, even the most radical, remains haunted by the ideal of a possible convergence of interests between white people and non-whites. In other words, it refuses to accept the possibility of a permanent racism. Sexton wasn't wrong to point out that this approach aligns with a Gramscian politics of hegemony: "political and organizational autonomy for the *indigènes*, and alliances with non-*indigènes* forces, integrating decolonial and anti-racist objectives, in the aim of constituting a majority of power."[137] The pessimism of Black radicalism has never believed in the feasibility of such an ambition. The idea that in a Western country a political majority could coalesce around the interests of Black people belongs to the realm of fantasy. This is why organizational autonomy was not only a means to an end, but already the beginning of the end. Realizing the power at the heart of Black nationalism or Pan-Africanism ultimately entailed their own undoing.

In contrast to this Black radicalism, and although it has never described itself in these terms, the political project of the Indigènes de la République has always been a radical multiculturalism. To "decolonize" France meant imagining a country where no dominant culture imposed itself over racial minorities. It meant imagining the end of all religious discrimination. It meant believing that, once a given community of foreign origin becomes the majority in a given territorial zone, it would hold political power and make its own rules prevail in accordance with its own democratic ambitions. And the rest of society would readily agree to this.

The notion of "racism" is misleading. It suggests that anti-Semitism, Islamophobia, Arabophobia, and anti-Blackness are all part of the same phenomenon. Between them, there is indeed a kinship, but they aren't the same. The discourse of "French exceptionalism" has done much to shape French thought. As the African American sociologist Crystal Marie Fleming has rightly pointed out, French discourse on race and racism tends to show a "penchant for trivializing the existence (or severity) of anti-black racism."[138] Due to its failed attempt at creating a settlers' colony in Algeria, its painful memory of the war that sealed its fate, and the demographic importance of the communities tied to this heritage, there is a widespread belief that, as Balibar has said, "Relations between France and Algeria, with their mutual sympathy and rivalries, are in their own way as impactful for our contemporary history as those between France and Germany."[139] Hence the priority given to anti-Arab racism in a national racial order very different from that of other slaveholding nations such as the United States or Britain. With the colonization of North Africa, anti-Arab racism has seemingly dwarfed anti-Blackness. This interpretation mistakenly takes the centrality of the North African point of view in anti-racist discourse as a reflection of the sociohistorical reality of the country. It stems from the successive achievements of Arab-majority organizations that have successfully raised awareness around Islamophobia, from the March of the 1980s to the present day. In particular, it has gained traction due to its ability to draw parallels between Islamophobia and anti-Semitism, which is always useful for arousing the residual guilt of the white left.

The reverse can be seen with Blackness in France. The scarcity of radical Afrodescendant voices in the French public sphere and the relative impotence of Black organizations are inversely proportional to the urgency and seriousness of the issues that concern them: the stubborn persistence of Françafrique and France's colonial policies in the West Indies and French Guiana – which Aimé Césaire described as early as 1975, before the French National Assembly, as "genocide by substitution"[140] and by persuasion. From an economic, geopolitical, and even libidinal perspective, anti-Blackness remains the resolute backbone of the French Empire. The lack of conversations on these issues isn't due to their subaltern position in relation to Maghrebi issues, but rather to an insufficient Black radical consciousness and politics in our current conjuncture. The foundations of this Black movement, however, are solid; it just needs to be expanded and strengthened. Indeed, while the Mouvement des Indigènes de la République emerged in 2005, so too did the Brigade Anti-Négrophobie [Anti-Black Racism Brigade], or BAN. Laying claim to the legacy of Black Power, the Black Panthers, and Black Consciousness as developed by Steve Biko, BAN articulates a more pessimistic stance regarding the permanence of anti-Black racism. Describing anti-Blackness as a hydra whose heads grow back as soon as they are cut off, it recounts how slavery evolved into the colonization of the African continent, and then:

> As soon as it was decapitated, the same viscerally anti-Black system grew back in the form of neo-colonialism, showing at times the paternalistic face of Françafrique, at others the condescending one of cooperation ... As the monstrous head of the Apartheid regime in South Africa has demonstrated, once cut off, anther grows back fast and strong, in the form of an economic apartheid ... imperceptible showcase of an even more daunting imperialism.[141]

In an approach in line with the tradition of Black pessimism, BAN seeks to develop a politics of empowerment and to awaken a deep cultural awareness, delivered from the temptation of meeting the enemy halfway.

BAN's politics, as articulated in its manifesto, is not necessarily at odds with that of the Indigènes – they have collaborated countless times since their respective founding – but it is expressed differently. This is because it is rooted in other experiences, in another history. It is not that these organizations should be pitted against one another – in no way are they competing against each other. But it should be noted that it is the political ontology that guides political perspectives and strategies, even though the dream of a harmonious convergence of interests between minorities remains desirable. Acknowledging differences doesn't preclude tactical coalitions and alliances. Such actions are needed to ensure decent conditions of survival for all descendants of slaves or colonized peoples. But the viability of the coalition depends on Black people's ability to avoid giving in to optimism and to remain focused on the reality of their condition and interests. Slavery is a part of them, regardless of the denials and objections. "Revolutionary love," Houria Bouteldja said, will save the indigènes. How can one not wish this for them? But Black people are condemned to revolutionary hate. Black lucidity is measured by its hatred of the world.[142]

Conclusion
Black Communism

I could have taken the usual European academic approach and offered a neutral, detached conclusion, a sort of scholastic synthesis, studded with critiques and well-placed counterpoints. In short, I could have demonstrated that I don't at all times agree with every idea – especially the most scandalous ones – articulated in the preceding pages, arguing in pedantic terms that reality is more complicated than a narrow focus on Black experience may imply, and that what is truly needed is a broader and more nuanced view. I am of the belief, though, that truth finds expression in *subtlety*, which is often an argument's most radical form, but it has little to do with *nuance*, which stems from fear of the consequences of its own conceptual demonstration. The pessimistic strain in contemporary African American theory is certainly not beyond critique. But the critique leveled at it so far is groundless: pessimism is quickly dismissed or pronounced scandalous without any real effort to understand it. My objective here has been to begin a frank discussion around these arguments and their theoretical consequences, without avoiding or minimizing any points of contention.

A central tenet of any contemporary political thought that claims to be revolutionary, progressive, or focused on equity is that Black people must begin by forgetting themselves. In interpretations of the Black radical tradition, it has become customary to emphasize, to the point of excluding all other matters, what has the least bearing on Black people themselves or their political interests. The sole focus is often on philanthropic acts and alliance building. The contemporary understanding of the history of the Black Panthers, including the regrettable Hollywood production of *Judas and the Black Messiah*, is emblematic of this approach. In leftist circles, the approach is often inflected with nostalgia for a Third Worldism devoid of any critical history. However, as the British sociologist Kehinde Andrews has written:

> The Third World movement offered a promise of a unified resistance to imperialism from the darker parts of the globe. ... By not rooting the politics around Blackness, the movement never safeguarded the interests of the Black people on the continent or in the Diaspora. The overt rejection of racialism is also one of the reasons why the movement became trapped in the colonial nation state.[1]

Coalition, alliance, and solidarity are no longer considered tools for mobilizing Black political power for the sake of just causes and human dignity on a wider scale. Instead, they are a coded order that calls for the self-annihilation of any Black organizing force. This is especially the case in the criticism leveled at Afropessimism from the left. In such an intellectual environment, it is hardly surprising that the British writer Annie Olaloku-Teriba saw it fit to end an article with an attack on Afropessimism, claiming that "the best that this politics can offer us is a fight without a purpose."[2] It is assumed and accepted that Black people, as a group with its own interests, either do not exist or are unworthy of attention.

We live in a world where the five poorest countries in terms of GDP per capita are in predominantly Black countries in Africa; a world where the poorest country in the western hemisphere is Haiti; a world where, in all the countries that practiced Black slavery, Black men are sent to prison at disproportionately higher rates than anyone else; a world where Black life expectancy is the lowest among all groups; a world where caricatural and humiliating representations of Africans are enjoyed to such an extent that they circulate, in extremely vile forms, even in Eastern and Central Europe or Asia – that is, in places with no history of anti-Black colonialism or slavery. These are but a few of the countless examples of the persistence of anti-Blackness discussed in this book. And, amid all this, critics of Afropessimism have no qualms writing that "the fragility of hierarchies of race is inherent to the project of racialism" and that "the 'blackness' of the category of slave was both contingent and unstable."[3] The constructivism of twentieth-century philosophy is today confused with the very structure of reality. By the sole act of writing that a historical phenomenon is "fragile," "constructed," or "unstable," one believes – notwithstanding all empirical evidence – one is directly seizing the hidden essence of reality. As conventional approaches to racism overlook the persistent critical state of Black masses throughout the world in favor of a shifting set of discourses and language games whereby one can track internal contradictions and changes with great amusement, anti-Blackness appears stripped of unity, coherence, and tenacity. The deliberate and constant ruin of Black people both within and outside of Africa is thus understood as an unfortunate set of circumstances, bound only to the vicissitudes of the development of the capitalist system.

Annie Olaloku-Teriba believes she is exempting Africans from the economy of Blackness by highlighting the role colonial governments played in consolidating ethnic categories.[4] This is akin to proving the futility of the category "cats" by pointing out the difference between a Siamese cat and a Persian cat. Blackness finds its coherence in the undifferentiated treatment of Black populations as disposable by former colonizers or new sub-Saharan potentates. Social death as described by Black pessimists is no mere fantasy or exaggeration. Nor is its aptness for depicting the contemporary condition of countless Africans a coincidence. In fact, others have described this condition in similar terms – such as the Congolese philosopher Kasereka Kavwahirehi, who is clearly more influenced by Jürgen Habermas and Ernst Bloch than by Saidiya Hartman and Tommy Curry: "The Great Lakes region of Africa is, literally speaking, a region of the bereaved, of the unburied, of the lawless, whose wandering souls, not understanding the fate that has been reserved for them until their death, come to haunt the city and the sleep of survivors."[5] Blackness isn't an ethnicity, nor even a phenotype: it is created out of the valuelessness assigned to lives of African descent by white people, people of color, or even Black people themselves. As Jared Sexton has rightly claimed:

> the emergent global apartheid, which primarily draws out of the picture the domestic black populations of the Americas (via the prison-industrial complex in the United States, ghettoization and displacement throughout the hemisphere) and the whole of sub-Saharan Africa (via structural adjustment programs), establishes the project of global civil society as uneven economic, political, and cultural integration along the East–West axis.[6]

One of the central tenets of African American pessimism is the idea that European political theories deemed progressive or revolutionary can sometimes be vehicles for anti-Blackness, other times indispensable tools for providing some relief to the Black condition, but that they are ill equipped to take on anti-Blackness as a global reality. Annie Olaloku-Teriba's critique is symptomatic of the paradigm inspired by Marxism and postmodernism. This is the dominant paradigm in the study of race, one that views skin color as a form of concealment. The antagonistic relation between Black and white people is but a smoke screen that masks a deeper and more important contradiction, that of class struggle. Following this line of thinking, any discussion about race is always really a discussion about class. In other words, racial difference, specific to colonial history, is but one manifestation of a class antagonism that permeates and structures history writ large. In this view, "race" or "Blackness" are merely names among others for the social contradiction that arises from the exploitation of labor. The Black feminist critic Hortense Spillers decisively shifted the terms of this debate, which we have yet to come fully to terms with.

The common-sense constructivist argument defines color as a superficial appearance that masks a greater unity of humankind. This is the ontological foundation of Karl Marx's famous remarks concerning America: "labor cannot emancipate itself in the white skin where in the black it is branded."[7] Though of different skin color, it is the *same* labor force, but only one is subjected to a more demeaning treatment. The distinction Marx makes is quantitative, not qualitative: work in Black skin is more stigmatized, but otherwise basically the same. Spillers doesn't dispute the idea that color conceals something, but what it hides for her is a *deeper difference*, not a similarity. The flesh of slaves or the colonized was radically marked by a history of trauma, experienced through torture, mutilation, and death: "These undecipherable markings on the captive body render a kind of hieroglyphics of the flesh whose severe disjunctures come to be hidden to the cultural seeing by skin color."[8] Our obsession with color drives us to neglect the deeper historicity of Blackness, its centuries-long connection with violence and dehumanization. In other words, our tendency to see Black difference as a difference in color has blinded us to the qualitative difference of white existence, whose need to dehumanize is all but ignored.

Black existence is defined by an abjection that can't be explained through the lens of labor and exploitation. Tommy Curry's Black Male Studies and the Afropessimism of Frank Wilderson and Jared Sexton both underscore the extent to which Black people are deeply marked by their status as the playthings of the white libidinal economy, as expendable objects in the white imaginary. The Marxist frame of reference, for its part, implies a commensurability between those who are exploited and those who are, in surplus, objects of cultural alienation, genocide, expropriation, and dehumanization. Black experience lies at the intersection of these phenomena, which explains why it doesn't fit within a Marxian analysis. This isn't because Marx was a victim of the racist clichés of his time (which has been said), but because his economic theory was simply not designed to grapple with anti-Blackness and the sort of struggles it provokes. To expect Marxism to give a definitive interpretation of the Black question makes no more sense than to expect geology to explain the functioning of the human brain.

However, many critiques of contemporary Black pessimism rely on the assumption that capitalism is the only globally structuring force, while race and Blackness are mere epiphenomena existing for a briefer span on a local scale. Black "progressive" thought has clearly inherited its terms and conceptual categories from the European social sciences, which prove of no help in understanding anti-Blackness. The only benefit for these thinkers is that this keeps open an easy and cordial dialogue with white thought. The popularity of the trendy notion "racial capitalism," with its intersectional buffet of options designed to satisfy all tastes, is thus in large part due to the permission it gives one to avoid dealing with singularities and particularities. The Black question thus becomes trapped and engulfed in the Caudine Forks of Marxism's crude categories. For this "progressive" thought, the aim is to recognize the importance of anti-Blackness for activists and intellectuals of African descent, but without making it a field of inquiry itself, which would require developing new analytical tools and concepts.

However, the African American political scientist Cedric Robinson, who coined the term *racial capitalism*, didn't share today's reservations toward Blackness. Praising its ability to counter both colonial rule and the bourgeois compradors and potentates of the postcolonial world, he defined the *Black radical tradition* as "the continuing development of a collective consciousness informed by the historical struggles for liberation and motivated by the shared sense of obligation to preserve the collective being, the ontological totality."[9] But this idea of an ontological dimension of Black collective belonging, a fundamental prerequisite of the radical tradition – though political ontology is defined in different terms by Robinson, by Hortense Spillers, by Afropessimists, by Black Male Studies – has largely been forgotten, censored, and foreclosed in the dominant constructivist tendencies of present-day critical theory where Marxism, with a poststructuralist bent, is given pride of place. There are deep divisions over the (rarely conceptualized) question of Black specificity. Recent critiques of this specificity in the context of Afropessimism are merely rehashing old arguments. In reality, the trial of Black nationalism and Pan-Africanism is perpetually rehearsed in the name of unity. "Marxism, the dominant form that the critique of capitalism has assumed in Western thought, incorporated theoretical and ideological weaknesses that stemmed from the same social forces that provided the bases of capitalist formation," writes Robinson in the opening pages of his seminal work *Black Marxism*.[10] This work, whose title should be read with irony, is not meant to be a contribution to Marxism but rather to Black thought and its specific radical tradition, incompatible with Marxism.

Huey Newton, the Black Panther Minister of Defense, claimed to be a dialectical materialist but refused the label of "Marxist." According to him, "a Marxist is someone who worships Marx and the thought of Marx. ... Such Marxists cherish the conclusions which Marx arrived at through his method, but they throw away the method itself – leaving themselves in a totally static posture."[11] What came to be known as "dialectical materialism" near the end of the nineteenth century is the product of a long history too often ignored or overly simplified. Generally, one thinks only of Hegel, Marx, or Lukács in connection with it, but its history goes back much further. It is present in the work of the pre-Socratic thinker Heraclitus,[12] and even in Aristotle,[13] who were themselves strongly informed by the teachings of the mystery schools of ancient Egypt.[14] This history also includes apocalyptic and gnostic religious traditions for which *the power of negation* was a central matter, and even embraces the Gospels themselves.[15] To focus solely on the Marxian moment of this trajectory limits its potential theoretical reach and insight.

One of the defining gestures of so-called "postmodernist" thought – from its emergence from poststructuralism in the second half of the twentieth century to today – has been to abolish the complexity of the tradition of dialectical philosophies. It was their impure origin – that is, their legacy beyond Marx – which led to their neglect. This is how, in his reading of Hegel, Althusser explained it. In reverence to the text of their master, Hegel, they kept the name of dialectic but erased the history behind it.[16] Going one step further, the "postmarxism" of Ernesto Laclau and Chantal Mouffe eliminated references to the dialectic altogether. From a centuries-long intellectual tradition, we seem to have retained nothing but Heraclitus' remark that "everything flows and nothing abides." In other words, contingency is the principle of all things. What was abolished, and remains ignored today, was the question of the negative – that is, the effort needed to change the course of history, which is not simply a varying flow devoid of consistency and solidity. The essence of dialectical thinking lies not in impermanence, but in understanding the world as governed by colossal powers and by the relationship established between these powers. The history of dialectical materialism is richer and deeper than its Marxist expression, in which Blacks will always be outsiders: generally tolerated, sometimes praised, but eternal novices and perpetual followers of European science. The best they can hope for is to have praise showered upon them for their virtuoso performance of a score written by someone else. Another score must be written. The point is not to renounce *Marxism*, but to renounce *being Marxist*. Only then will one become a communist better positioned to respond to the challenges of anti-Blackness.

Wilderson has inherited poststructuralism's skepticism of dialectics, which explains his ill-considered hostility toward it and his reduction of it to a form of naive optimism. It also explains his profound misunderstanding of the South African theorist and activist Steve Biko, whose work, based on the politicization of the Black consciousness, is key to laying a new foundation for a Black Communism.[17] Marxists made Marxism–Leninism a science, not because it seemed like a plausible undertaking, but because it was part of a strategy for constructing new political subjects. The idea of crystallizing Marxist discourse in a science, and then making this universalizable, would allow everyone – proletariat and disaffected petty-bourgeois alike – to embrace the cause of the working class. This is not out of a magnanimous spirit, but because this commitment is consistent with a rigorous and scientific reading of history and its trajectory. Black Communism need not depend on this ruse. Black consciousness is consciousness of a consciousness; it is a matter of knowing oneself as oppressed and dehumanized, of finding new ways to reconnect with a long tradition of abolitionist, Black nationalist, anti-colonialist, Pan-African philosophy and activism, which has been fueled by inhabiting this reality.

However, critiques of Afropessimism have rightly called attention to the paradigm's lack of historical rigor and its partial reading of Black political history. Annie Olaloku-Teriba and Pan-Africanist Greg Thomas have been outspoken critics of its tendency to reduce Black history to its North American version. They also contest its problematic notion that Blacks in the New World lost all traces of Africanness as a result of being enslaved.[18] But interpreting the slave ship as a *tabula rasa* of race isn't characteristic of Afropessimism. A strong version of it can be found in the work of the Martinican writer and critic Édouard Glissant, according to whom the African population of the West Indies, reduced to slavery, "has not brought with it, not collectively continued, the methods of existence and survival, both material and spiritual, which it practiced before being uprooted. These methods leave only dim traces or survive in the form of spontaneous impulses."[19] This rupture, this absence of an existential tangibility of Afrodescendants, provides the basis for Glissant's apology of hybridity, which he calls "creolization." This Creole anti-essentialism, largely motivated by the rejection of Aimé Césaire's Négritude, is widely influential and doesn't provoke the same repulsion as Afropessimism. The leader of the radical left in France, Jean-Luc Mélenchon, even incorporated it into his political platform.[20] If, despite its unmistakable rupture with Africanness, Creolism provokes less repulsion than Afropessimism, it is because the issue at stake in Creolism is not its wish to preserve a reference to Africa, nor a question of rupture or continuity between sub-Saharans and the diaspora. Rather, its favorable reception is due to its promotion of a hybrid and malleable conception of the political subject, which entails abolishing the name "Black," seen now as a hindrance to politics and thought.

In reality, and as opposed to Glissant, Afropessimists do not claim there is any radical rupture between Africa and the diaspora, but reverse the way this relationship is most often framed. Usually, when an effort is made to bridge the two sides of the Atlantic, African traditions provide the basis for an analysis of African American culture. Afropessimists flip this on its head, asking us to use Black slavery as the basis for rethinking modern and contemporary Africa. Continental Africans should be seen not as descendants of accomplices of white enslavers, but as occupying a place in a global order where Black people, regardless of their origin, exist as potential slaves. What matters most, then, is no longer identity or culture, but the ripple effects of the Black Atlantic slave trade on the entirety of the global Afrodescendant populations, which were thrust into dehumanization. This phenomenon, instead of being interpreted as the antithesis of Pan-Africanism, could be conceived as a decisive step in reinventing its intellectual and political legacy, which I'm calling Black Communism. As Wilderson writes, "Blacks ... cannot claim their bodies, cannot claim their families, cannot claim their cities, cannot claim their countries, they cannot lay claim to a personal pronoun. [Africa] is (or was, sticking with the diaspora) no more 'their continent' than the slave cabin was 'their home.'"[21] To be clear, it isn't a question here of renouncing Africa, but of renouncing the idea that Black people can find salvation by rediscovering some sort of mystical, telluric, or primordial, connection with Africa. Africa could be the place where this politics emerges – a politics free of all ideals of autochthony, of blind patriotism, of indigenism, realizing, at last, "the landless inhabitation of selfless existence."[22] The Haitian Revolution offered the first promise of this. It is thus a matter of rethinking Africa in political terms, not as the origin of Black people, but as their destination. A place where they have everything to gain, including their own humanity.

Contemporary Black pessimistic thinking has been seen as a betrayal of the Black radical tradition because what people have taken away from it is only the part that is compatible with non-Black progressivism, be it Marxist, Third Worldist, liberal, or postmodern. But Afropessimism and Black Male Studies have furthered the Black radical tradition more than they have strayed from it. Rather than break with the Black political legacy, they invite us to revisit it with a renewed appreciation of its two founding observations: first, that a vast portion of white societies harbor an unshakable hostility toward African populations, and, second, that this hostility has become a key element of their political theories and philosophies, whose principles and approaches can only be appropriated at the cost of a profound transformation, guided by Black interests. Essentially, though, the best approach is to carve out a new path. It would be criminal or unconscionable today to adopt a naive apology of capitalism as did Marcus Garvey in the first half of the twentieth century. But his critique of white communism remains pertinent: "The greatest enemies of the Negro are among those who hypocritically profess love and fellowship for him, when, in truth, and deep down in their hearts, they despise and hate him. Pseudo-philanthropists and their organizations are killing the Negro."[23] The aim of Black Communism is to articulate a social project centered on Black dignity, derived from the histories, experiences, and philosophies of Africans and Afrodescendants, taking care to keep their interests as the focal point. This will require, for example, a renewed critique of private property, such as that outlined by Rinaldo Walcott, which makes a case for the relevance of anti-slavery abolitionism to our present moment: "Abolition has come to occupy the place that the promise of communism once held for many of us. ... We do not just want to abolish the police and the courts; we want to abolish everything."[24] Unlike Walcott, I believe there is still value in the notion of communism. But he is right to ground a new radical critique of property in the shared experiences of the diaspora, not just in the mechanics of exploitation as described by Marx: "The precarity produced by the government's withdrawal of key social services is then made a part of the criminalization continuum. It is these conditions that the abolition of property means to interrupt, and in so doing change the fundamental conditions and priorities of our collective future."[25]

Just as class struggle doesn't necessarily mean solidarity should be sought among *all* workers – fascists being a case in point – Black Communism, whose politics are based on the fundamental fact of dehumanization, need not accommodate *all* Black people: no exceptions can be made for the Black *lumpenbourgeoisie*, African neo-colonialist governments, and other enemies of the Black masses. To turn Stuart Hall's famous claim on its head, "class is the modality by which race is experienced." For race determines whether one belongs to humanity, and class describes the social conditions of that (non)belonging. In other words, the question of class is of decisive importance *within the confines of Blackness*. Kwame Nkrumah and Julius Nyerere did much to highlight African communalist traditions to legitimize their African socialist ambitions. But to no avail, largely due to the fact that these African socialisms failed to appreciate the class stratification of the newly independent countries. The takeaway from this history is not that these specific iterations of African socialism should be abandoned altogether, but that we should go further, that we should demand more of ourselves. Black Communism must reassess these histories with a critical eye in order to come up with new projects, new strategies, new sets of beliefs.

Black thought and politics cannot depend on collaborating with groups that don't consider Black people fully human. It is for this reason that the present order must be abolished and a new radical politics established. Countless contortions have been made throughout history – and will continue to be made – to evade this simple truth. By confusing Black interests with those of the citizen or the proletariat, liberalism and Marxism stand as two serious obstacles on the road to intellectual and political independence for the Blacks of the world. As Steve Biko emphasized, the power of white racism "works with unnerving totality, featuring both on the offensive and in our defense."[26] Any political program that relegates the Black question to the background participates in this all-consuming totality. Countering it thus requires that Black people embrace their specificity,[27] beginning by relinquishing the belief that they belong to humanity like any other, in a world that does not treat them accordingly. More important still, it involves what Biko calls "power politics,"[28] which is the catalyst for Black Communism.

Biko saw clearly that the only way to fight anti-Blackness was not to abandon the Black condition in favor of some diverse coalition – where anti-Blackness finds a diversity of expression – but rather to invest this condition with all the power possible. Or, to put it in Richard Wright's words, to militarize it.[29] One may object that Biko's Blackness was also open to people of color who were not of African descent. But even the Black Liberation Army, a direct-action group in the United States in the 1970s, had a significant white contingent. Why not welcome that? Indeed, what matters is that Black lives, names, and interests are staunchly positioned at the center of this thinking and activism. Only under these conditions does a deep love for one's own people and a genuine hatred of the world – the two prerequisites for abolishing the appalling totality unfolding before us – take shape. Pessimism awakens at the dawn of Black dignity.

Postface
The Conceptual Limitations of
Studying Blackness
Tommy J. Curry

The contemporary debates over the meaning of
Blackness – what Blackness is, what Blackness consequences are, what violence Blackness causes – have
followed disciplinary dogma rather than the realities
of Black death, Black disadvantage, and wretchedness
that dictates the reality of Black people in America.
Black Studies has produced several abstractions
concerning Blackness that have come to dictate our
current academic discourse. Black Studies began with
the intent to decolonize the way that theory relates to
reality. For Black sociologists such as Nathan Hare,
who founded Black Studies at San Francisco State in
1968, the study of Black people required a decolonizing
effort that replaces the assumptions about the Blackness
imposed by the categories of white science with studies
creating endemic conceptual schemas. "Decolonization
is the process by which the oppressed group begins to
determine its own destiny and run its own affairs ...
A genuine decolonization effort requires breaking the
psychological, cultural, political and economic shackles
of the old order," writes Hare.[1] Black Studies requires
a reformulation of the very ideas and categories of
thought, as if we are encountering a new being for
the very first time. The abstraction's relationship with

reality finds itself in the inexplicable, not the predetermined or presumed.

Despite the allusion to radicality and the presumed distance Black theory has from the set orders of Western knowledge, the abstractions of Blackness that dictate our current academic discourse depend on the substitution of the humanity of disowned Black bodies for theoretical recognition. Our current theories use Blackness as a platform upon which Black bodies are tried and convicted as the least desirable Black subgroup. Blackness presents itself as the basis of wretchedness; however, the ongoing practice of assigning privilege and power to oppressed groups within Blackness has created a mechanism through which the theories of Blackness afford recognition to some bodies and deny it to others. Racist caricatures concerning violence, intellectual inferiority, and savagery apply to the most undesirable Black population. These Black bodies, which are often Black and male, poor and uneducated, and thought to be violent, are conceptually placed beyond the bounds of theory and recognition. Theory makes Black males objects of others' thoughts – abject and absent. Within disciplines, theory is deployed in the service of creating hierarchies among Black people and attributing the victimization of racist horrors among the most recognizable Black bodies. Consequently, our analyses of Blackness seek to ground recognition in the horrid. On the one hand, Blackness marks the condition of a population marked for death, whom theory describes as fungible, the slave, and negated. On the other hand, theory allows certain Black bodies to be marked with the attributes of savagery and barbarism so much so that they are conceptualized as threats to other Blacks, such as Black women, Black children, or Black sexual minorities. These Black males, conceptualized as most savage, most dangerous, the most unfit for civil society, are the bodies permanently stained by Blackness. These

Black bodies cursed by their phallic flesh – burdened by the attributes of the beast, the pathology of the Nigger – remain confined to an ongoing dehumanization making recognition within Western societies impossible.

The violence, poverty, and societal deprivation enacted against Black Americans have generated various conceptual theories aiming to explain the perpetual states of dehumanization that accompany the stain of Blackness. Afro-pessimists have laid claim to the position of the slave to capture the gratuitous violence directed toward Black bodies within a white supremacist society. The problem of dehumanization continues to burden Black folks while simultaneously giving a privileged class of Black academics the ability to commodify Black suffering as academic currency. The Black bodies who are thought to be more assimilable to the liberal categories of white disciplines become the subject positions thought to be acceptable for theorization. Just as Sylvia Wynter has explained that the truly wretched, those liminal populations enduring both societal ostracization and lethal violence, are beyond the interest of academics because they are beyond the reach of theory, theory rewards *theorizable* Black bodies so that they can be seen and believed to be distant from those trapped by their pathological Blackness in the ghettos, prisons, and poverty.[2]

Black Male Studies and the Disaggregation of Violence and Death Affecting Black People

Black Male Studies refuses the temptation to ascend into white recognition through an articulation of Black death as a call for white conscience and reward. Philosophically, the study of the Black male and his relation to other racialized males who have suffered the terror of genocide, the mutilation of the corpse through war, and the violence of castration forces Black consciousness inward so that it can understand the conceptual architecture responsible for the institutions and practices of social order which depend on the Black male corpse. Black Male Studies insists upon the disaggregation of violence imposed upon Black people. Overwhelmingly, the disadvantage and violence associated with anti-Black racism are imposed upon Black males in the United States. Black men make up roughly 96 percent of the Black victims killed by police in the United States.[3] Despite being the majority of Black victims, Black men are theorized as privileged by their dying at the hands of police officers. Intersectional theorists assert that Black male death occupies too central a position in how the world thinks about police violence and is privileged over other Black groups who are killed significantly less than Black men.[4] To de-emphasize the victimization and death of Black males, the recognition of Black male suffering is interpreted as oppressive and marginalizing to less victimized groups.

Multiple social scientific studies have confirmed that being a Black male disproportionately increases one's exposure to violence and risk of premature death, compared to other race/sex groups in the United States. Being Black and male significantly increases the risk that an individual will have a lethal engagement with police officers in the United States.[5] In the mind of whites, Black men are more associated with danger and criminality than their female counterparts. Some studies have found that femaleness deactivates the racial stereotypes and has a protective function regarding the propensity whites have to shoot Black people. These studies show that educated whites are more likely to shoot unarmed Black men than they are to shoot armed Black or white women.[6] The deleterious effects of Blackness, being disproportionately comprised of Black male death and disadvantage, extend far beyond the problem of police violence. The wealth gap between Blacks and whites in the United States is largely the effect of the downward economic mobility and lack of employment imposed upon Black men.[7] Additionally, Black men have the lowest life expectancy and are the race/sex group most at risk for premature death in the US.[8] Liberal arts theorists deliberately ignore the intra-racial violence against Black men and the rates of intimate partner victimization and sexual assault that refute the idea that Black men are primarily perpetrators of domestic violence and sexual assault in the Black community. Black men are more likely than all groups of men and most groups of women to experience intimate partner violence victimization,[9] dating violence,[10] reproductive coercion and control,[11] made-to-penetrate violence,[12] and intimate partner homicide.[13]

Our current theories have overdetermined Black men and boys as perpetrators of violence and the animating forces of intraracial maleficence. In other words, Black males are required to be conceptualized as violent subjects who harm other Black people to maintain the idea that other marginalized Black groups are harmed by Blackness. From Afropessimism to intersectionality, the theories used to motivate Black Studies require a peculiar mythopoesis that demands Black males to be invented.[14] Black males are fictive characters driven by anti-social behavior and pathological ideations for harm in most cutting-edge theories of Blackness. While the imagination of the Black theories is presumed to be earnest, it is influenced by the interiorization of anti-Blackness that remains in the world and resides in the Black consciousness. The implication of Wynter's reflection on the sociogenic principle is that the categories and fictions of the white mind become the negations in Black consciousness.[15] The Black male is presented to the Black mind as the problem of Black being. He is the terror that should not exist but needs to exist so that disciplinary theories of Blackness can explain why marginalized identities (e.g., the woman, the queer, the trans, the child, etc.) are oppressed by his very existence. Black males are denied victimization, not because we do not have ample evidence of the harm they suffer from other Black people in their communities, but because the violent threats they are conceptualized to be are required to give meaning to the theories pretending to give a correct explanation of Black death – its causes and ultimate end.

The milieu of death and negativity surrounding Black men in the United States is not only political and social but academic and theoretical. Practically every journalistic or academic endeavor represents Black men through their corpses and deviance. In such a world, I am inspired to ask: "How does one *think* Black men?" The Black man is claimed to be known with little to no actual studying of his attitudes, experiences, or suffering. Consequently, he is cast as a problem of thought – assumed to be the burden from which all other identities must be freed. As a problem of thought, he is to be removed from *thinking* and represented as that which inhibits theory. If thinking is an activity by which the mind grasps and abstracts from the phenomenological world a concept or phantasm of the object observed, it would be reasonable to say that Black men are unthought, because they are concretized in the mind as that which they *are* in the world. In this sense, there is synonymity between what Black males are *thought to be* and what they *are* in the world, because they resist theoretical approach.

Rethinking Black Thought

Racism is a mechanism of dehumanization. It requires the subjugation and death of the racialized population for the enrichment and benefit of the dominant white group. Previously, I have argued that anti-Black racism in America "is a complex nexus, a cognitive architecture used to invent, reimagine, and evolve the presumed political, social, economic, sexual, and psychological superiority of the white races in society, while materializing the imagined inferiority and hastening the death of inferior races."[16] The managing of dissident racial populations requires the dominant racial group to provide a logics and rationalization for the need to segregate or exterminate the subordinate racial group. These logics are the objects of theoretical investigation and the basis of positive conceptualizations of Blackness aimed to resist the caricatures of dehumanization. If one understands racism to be "the manifestation of the social processes and concurrent logics that facilitate the death and dying of racially subjugated peoples," then our theories of racism should consider the societal and demographic consequences of the worldview that dominant groups deploy against Blacks to realize a world where Black existence is of little consequence. As the late Derrick Bell once said, "we have never understood that the essence of the racism we contended against was not simply that we were exploited in slavery, degraded by segregation, and frustrated by the unmet promises of equal opportunity. The essence of racism in America was the hope that we who were [B]lack would not exist."[17] Reorienting racism and our analysis of Blackness around the material effects (the empirical realities) of anti-Black violence and degradation extricates *thought* from academic *theory*.

Racism vacates Blackness of any positive or self-determined meaning. It despises Black existence and prefers caricature. In this reality, Black people can be recognized as human only insofar as they are deputized and consigned in the larger war against Black savagery. Philosophy in Europe and America is being confronted by the voices emanating from horizons beyond its geography of reason. These voices announce a limitation and border of thought. However, within the social organization of practically all white societies, managed by political asymmetry between racial and ethnic groups, and economic divisions that refuse data-driven disaggregation, what hope does an uninformed appeal to racial remediation through tolerance, democracy, or even decolonization have in the world? Blackness is a rupture and can serve as a starting point of philosophical reflection that begins with the problematization and rejection of the humanist orientation of philosophical thought. The universalization of the European and Euro-American experience requires abstractions that are alien to Black reality. The late Charles Mills explained that "The peculiar features of the African-American experience – racial slavery, which linked biological phenotype to social subordination, and which is chronologically located in the modern epoch, ironically coincident with the emergence of liberalism's proclamation of universal human equality – are not part of the experience represented in the abstractions of European or Euro-American philosophers."[18]

Despite decades of philosophical reflection and argumentative refutations questioning the starting point of philosophical inquiry, philosophy remains committed to pursuing a Eurocentric and universalist view of reason as the structure and force of its endeavors. The subhuman position described throughout "Non-Cartesian sums" by Mills insists that philosophical practice cannot presume the intuitive or shared communality of the human as an endeavor. Sub-personhood is an organizing concept throughout Mills' work, a construct aiming to show "that white racism so structured the world as to have negative ramifications for every sphere of black life – juridical standing, moral status, personal/racial identity, epistemic reliability, existential plight, political inclusion, social metaphysics, sexual relations, aesthetic worth."[19] The human – the abstract that provides a grounding for humanity – simply cannot answer the problem introduced by Mills, and most recently answered by the political nihilist Calvin Warren. If Blackness / Black *being* renders one outside of humanity, and the Black is not a human being, "then on what bases can we assert the mattering of Black existence?" asks Warren.[20]

The disciplinary apparatus of philosophy has made the aim of decolonization pseudological – or what I defined in "On derelict and method" as a form of criticism that embraces those discourses, techniques, and tactics that respect the recently emergent humanity of whites as the condition of our inclusion within philosophy. Pseudological criticism often seems to be radical in its rhetorical style but ultimately appeals to disciplinary philosophy for entrance into the haloed halls of recognition. Earlier in my career, I understood this form of criticism to be the basis by which Black historical figures and contemporary scholars were allowed entrance into philosophy. While this is certainly the case, there is also an affective dimension to the philosophical enterprise that requires some comment. To be philosophical renders the criticism of philosophy a mediation between what has been the historical brutality and the contemporary denial of racism's effect on not only the political and social organization of European and American societies, but also the pretense that racism can be engaged objectively, neutrally, and without the presence of the Black bodies and thoughts still excluded from the field itself. It is this absence of Black people and Black thought that allows decolonization and the problem of racism to be framed as a political problem requiring a new etiquette, rather than thinking of Blackness and the problem of Blackness as a window into new generative concepts concerning the world and the social reality we are currently shackled to as the foundation of our current thinking. Dr. Norman Ajari's new work makes great strides in responding to the absence of the pessimism of Black thought in Black political theory. Philosophy marginalizes the prominence of pessimism throughout Black intellectual history by condemning Black nationalism, demonizing Black militancy, and erasing Black males, who have for centuries rejected the aspirations of American and European democracy.

A Novel Contribution to Black Philosophy and Decolonial Thought

The debates over Blackness are complex, ideological, and a political minefield in the American academy. *Darkening Blackness* is a corrective to the seemingly endless pessimistic trends throughout contemporary Black theories that are designated as Afropessimism. Not distracted by the popular ideas of our time, Dr. Ajari brings clarity to the tomes of despair that motivate Black Studies. The death of Black people and the political order demanding their silence and acquiescence in the face of their subjugation require theorists to dare to think beyond our political and disciplinary confines. It is in the service of Black thought to escape the limitations of our time, and Dr. Ajari's book refuses to be confined by the consensus of our current day. He challenges us to embrace pessimism through the actualization of Black radicality. He demands that Black thought fulfill its duty to Black life without spiraling into the despair of Black death.

"Being Black means being condemned to live and die as another's fantasy," writes Ajari. Black radical thought refuses the ontological entailment of epistemic problems. It is pessimism that ignites resistance to this peculiar grammar of white supremacist society. The political movements that manifested themselves as Black Power, and even Black Studies, introduced a new concept of the human. The Black human does not exist in society or the white imaginary. Ajari understands that the violence of anti-Black racism is that it sequestrates the Black soul from Black bodies. These Black bodies are represented as voids, conceptualized as empty vessels, only capable of being satiated through the recognition of their plight within theory and by the very white institutions and individuals responsible for their oppression in the first place. Ajari intervenes in the disciplinary contests that allow white theorists to celebrate the defeatism of Black pessimism as a white triumph. By centering the struggles of Black radicals and indigenous folk, Ajari gives pause to the political ideations which insist upon less reflective thinking. This is why his proposal of Black Communism, which is a product of the reflective Black conscious, offers such a powerful positive program of engaging the negations of the white world. According to Ajari, "The proposal of a Black Communism aims to formulate a project of society founded centrally on black dignity, from the histories, experiences and philosophies of Africans and Afro-descendants, in order to be as close as possible to their interests." Unlike the previous critiques of Afropessimism as merely a diagnostic that aims to destroy the world, Ajari proposes the destruction of the white world through the conditions that make the reconstitution of a Black world actualizable.

Contrary to the retreat from Blackness as a political and epistemological – or philosophical – posture, Ajari disregards the distractions of essentialist charges and elucidates the power of Biko's Black Consciousness. Just as Biko understood the need to refute the inferiority complex of the Black mind through reauthorizing the grammar of Black being, so too does Ajari reclaim

Blackness (and the pessimism founded upon the subhumanity of those who are Black) as a universe that provides the normative and axiological possibility of philosophically grounding itself. This gesture does not accept the negations of Blackness as purely metaphysical, but allows Blacks to claim Blackness for themselves.[21] *Darkening Blackness* covers an impressive and broad conceptual terrain and offers an energizing and novel take on the failures of academic theory to speak to Black life amidst the burden of Black death in the United States.

Notes

Introduction: Centrality and Erasure of Black Pessimism

1 Russell Vought, "M-20-34," 2020: www.whitehouse.gov/wp-content/uploads/2020/09/M-20-34.pdf.
2 Center For Renewing America: https://americarenewing.com/issue_topic/critical-race-theory.
3 Presidential Documents, "Combatting sex and race stereotyping," *Federal Register*, no. 188, vol. 85, 2020, p. 60683.
4 Stéphanie Le Bars, "La 'critical race theory,' nouvel avatar de la guerre culturelle aux États-Unis," *Le Monde*, July 2, 2021.
5 Daniel Trilling, "Why is the UK government suddenly targeting 'Critical Race Theory'?" *The Guardian*, October 23, 2020.
6 Paul Warmington, "'A tradition in ceaseless motion': Critical Race Theory and Black British intellectual spaces," *Race, Ethnicity and Education*, 15, 1, 2012, p. 19.
7 *Translator's note*: The connotations of *indigène* in French are distinct from those of its English counterpart, *indigenous*. It is hard to consider the term outside the context of French colonial history and its varied set of oppressive policies, known as the *Code de l'indigénat*. Its reappropriation is meant to evoke the legacy and continuity of this colonial history. For this reason, I have left the term untranslated throughout this work.
8 Anne-Sophie Nogaret, "La hallalisation des esprits," *Causeur*, 53, 2018, p. 53.
9 Irène Ahmadi, "Macron juge le 'monde universitaire coupable' d'avoir 'cassé la République en deux,'" *Les Inrocks*, June 11, 2020.
10 Qtd. in Chris Moody, "How critical race theory overran the

Southern Baptist Convention," *New York Magazine*, June 16, 2021.

11 Tommy J. Curry, "Racism and the equality delusion: the real CRT," Institute of Arts and Ideas, July 16, 2021.

12 Qtd. in Berthony DuPont, *Jean-Jacques Dessalines: itinéraire d'un révolutionnaire* (Paris: L'Harmattan, 2006), pp. 261–2.

13 Baron de Vastey, *The Colonial System Unveiled*. Trans. Chris Bongie (Liverpool University Press, 2014).

14 W. E. B. Du Bois, "On being ashamed of oneself: an essay on race pride," *The Crisis*, 40, 9, Sept. 1933, p. 200.

15 Aimé Césaire, "Nègrerie. Conscience raciale et révolution sociale" (1935), *Écrits politiques: 1935–1956* (Paris: Jean-Michel Place, 2016), p. 33.

16 Alphonso Pinkney, *The Myth of Black Progress* (Cambridge University Press, 1984), p. 16.

17 Tommie Shelby, *We Who Are Dark* (Cambridge, MA: Harvard University Press, 2007), pp. 6–7.

18 Cornel West, "On Black nationalism," in *The Cornel West Reader* (New York: Civitas Books, 1999), pp. 528–9.

19 Alphonso Pinkney, *Red, Black, and Green: Black Nationalism in the United States* (Cambridge University Press, 1976), p. 28.

20 Jennifer C. Nash, *Black Feminism Reimagined: After Intersectionality* (Durham, NC: Duke University Press, 2019), p. 22.

1 The Sources of the Afropessimist Paradigm

1 Manning Marable, *Beyond Black and White: From Civil Rights to Barack Obama* (London: Verso Books, 2016), p. 116.

2 Frank B. Wilderson III, *Afropessimism* (New York: Liveright, 2020), pp. 14–15. Wilderson's emphasis.

3 Greg Thomas, "Afro-Blue Notes: The Death of Afro-Pessimism (2.0)?" *Theory & Event*, 21, 1, 2018, pp. 282–317.

4 Stephen Smith, *Négrologie: Pourquoi l'Afrique se meurt* (Paris: Calmann-Lévy, 2003); J.-P. Chrétien et al., "Misères de l'afro-pessimisme," *Afrique & Histoire*, 3, 1, 2001, pp. 183–211.

5 Sony Labou Tansi, *Encre, sueur, salive & sang* (Paris: Seuil, 2015), p. 136.

6 Kwame Nkrumah, *Neocolonialism: The Last Stage of Imperialism* (London: Thomas Nelson & Sons, 1965).

7 Saidiya V. Hartman and Frank B. Wilderson III, "The position of the unthought," *Qui Parle*, 13, 2, 2003, p. 197.

8 Tommy J. Curry, "Africana philosophy: the development of the discipline in the United States," *Choice*, 54, 9, May 2017, n.p.

9 Derrick Bell, *Faces at the Bottom of the Well: The Permanence of Racism* (New York: Basic Books, 1992), p. 12.

10 Derrick Bell, *Silent Covenants: Brown vs. Board of Education and the Unfulfilled Hopes for Racial Reform* (Oxford University Press, 2005), p. 198.

11 Richard Delgado and Jean Stefancic, *Critical Race Theory: An Introduction* (New York University Press, 2012), p. 37.

12 David T. Goldberg, *Are We All Postracial Yet?* (Cambridge: Polity, 2015), p. 39.

13 Tommy J. Curry, "Canonizing the Critical Race artifice: an analysis of philosophy's gentrification of Critical Race Theory," in P. C. Taylor, L. M. Alcoff, and L. Anderson (eds.), *The Routledge Companion to the Philosophy of Race* (New York: Routledge, 2017), p. 356.

14 Bell, *Silent Covenants*, p. 198.

15 See, for example, Frank B. Wilderson III, *Red, White & Black: Cinema and the Structure of U.S. Antagonisms* (Durham, NC: Duke University Press, 2010), p. 84; Jared Sexton, "People-of-color-blindness: notes on the afterlife of slavery," *Social Text*, 28, 2, 2010, p. 32; Calvin L. Warren, *Ontological Terror: Blackness, Nihilism, and Emancipation* (Durham, NC: Duke University Press, 2018), pp. 50–1.

16 Giorgio Agamben, *"What Is an Apparatus?" and Other Essays*. Trans. David Kishik and Stefan Pedatella (Stanford University Press, 2009).

17 Giorgio Agamben, *The Signature of All Things: On Method*. Trans. Luca di Santo and Kevin Attell (New York: Zone Books, 2009), p. 31.

18 *Ibid.*, p. 29.

19 Giorgio Agamben, *Potentialities: Collected Essays in Philosophy*. Ed. and trans. Daniel Heller-Roazen (Stanford University Press, 1999), p. 93. Just as Walter Benjamin claimed to borrow Carl Schmitt's approach in *Political Theology*, transferring it from the philosophy of the State to that of art, Agamben exports Warburg's philosophy of art to the realm of political and social theory.

20 Agamben, *The Signature of All Things*, p. 22.

21 *Ibid.*, p. 32.

22 Giorgio Agamben, *Homo sacer: Sovereign Power and Bare Life*. Trans. Daniel Heller-Roazen (Stanford University Press, 1998), p. 8.

23 *Ibid.*, p. 128. Agamben's emphasis.

24 Giorgio Agamben, *Means without End: Notes on Politics*. Trans. Cesare Casarino and Vincenzo Binetti (Minneapolis: University of Minnesota Press, 2000), p. 10.

25 Giorgio Agamben, *The Highest Poverty: Monastic Rules and Form-of-Life*. Trans. Adam Kotsko (Stanford University Press, 2011), p. 29.

26 This closely reproduces and extends the thinking of Guy Debord, who, in his film *Critique de la séparation*, states that "the question isn't to note that people live more or less in poverty, but always in a manner that escapes them." Georges Bataille expressed this in similar terms, writing that "slavery brings into the world the absence of light that is the separate positing of each *thing*, reduced to the *use* it has": Georges Bataille, *The Accursed Share: An Essay on General Economy*. Trans. Robert Hurley (New York: Zone Books, 1991), p. 57. Bataille's emphasis.

27 See Judith Butler and Gayatri Spivak, *Who Sings the Nation-State? Language, Politics, Belonging* (London: Seagull Books, 2011), p. 17.

28 Giorgio Agamben, *Where Are We Now? The Epidemic as Politics*. Trans. Valeria Dani (Lanham, MD: Rowman & Littlefield, 2021).

29 Orlando Patterson, *Slavery and Social Death: A Comparative Study* (Cambridge, MA and London: Harvard University Press, 1982).

30 Jared Sexton, "The social life of social death: on Afropessimism and Black optimism," *InTensions*, 5, 2011, p. 29. Sexton's emphasis.

31 It should be noted that the notion of social death as used by Afropessimist thinkers has undergone its own shift in meaning. The term originated in the work of the French anthropologist Claude Meillassoux, for whom it referred specifically to the *capture* of slaves and their experience of death in regard to the society, traditions, and customs into which they were born, before being thrust into a new society where they occupied a subaltern position. Afropessimism enacts a shift in its meaning by focusing more on the historically unique – or almost – situation in the antebellum South in the United States where the reproduction of slaves was through birth, rather than through the constant renewal of an adult labor force as is generally the case in slave contexts. See Norman Ajari, *Dignity or Death: Ethics and Politics of Race*. Trans. Matthew B. Smith (London: Polity, 2022), pp. 187–8.

32 Wilderson III, *Red, White & Black*, p. 11.

33 Afropessimist analysis is rooted in the historical analysis of Orlando Patterson, for whom it is not incidental that slavery coincides with economic development and cultural refinement in art and literature – as was the case in ancient Greece and Rome, in the Ottoman Empire, and all of the Mediterranean world, or even in the Americas of the eighteenth and nineteenth centuries. In fact, by freeing up time for the master class, slavery makes these developments possible. Afropessimists offer an ontological reading of this argument by replacing the figure of the slave, of varying ethnicity historically, with that of the Black man or woman.

34 Hortense J. Spillers, *Black, White and in Color: Essays on American Literature and Culture* (University of Chicago Press, 2003), p. 215. Spiller's emphasis.

35 Shannon Winnubst, "The many lives of fungibility: anti-Blackness in neoliberal times," *Journal of Gender Studies*, 29, 1, 2020, p. 104.

36 bell hooks, *Ain't I a Woman: Black Women and Feminism* (New York and London: Routledge, 2015), p. 9.

37 Tommy J. Curry, *The Man-Not: Race, Class, Genre, and the Dilemmas of Black Manhood* (Philadelphia: Temple University Press, 2017), p. 55.

38 hooks, *Ain't I a Woman*, p. 13.

39 Curry, *The Man-Not*, pp. 58–9.

40 Saidiya V. Hartman, *Scenes of Subjection: Terror, Slavery, and Self-Making in Nineteenth-Century America* (Oxford and New York: Oxford University Press, 1997), p. 100.

41 bell hooks, *Feminism Is for Everybody: Passionate Politics* (Cambridge, MA: South End Press, 2000), p. 17.

42 Michele Wallace, "A Black feminist's search for sisterhood," *But Some of Us Are Brave: Black Women's Studies* (New York: The Feminist Press at CUNY, 1982).

43 Wilderson III, *Red, White & Black*, p. 89.

44 Spillers, *Black, White and in Color*, p. 207.

45 Hartman, *Scenes of Subjection*, p. 22.

2 Theoretical Origins of Afropessimism

1 My description of these two dimensions of anti-Black violence – scale and intensity – draws on what the philosopher Étienne Balibar has called ultra-objective and ultra-subjective violence: Étienne Balibar, *La crainte des masses: politique et philosophie avant et après Marx* (Paris: Galilée, 1997), p. 44.

2 Guillaume Hervieux, *L'ivresse de Noé: histoire d'une malediction* (Paris: Perrin, 2011), p. 48.

3 Chouki El Hamel, *Black Morocco: A History of Slavery, Race, and Islam* (Cambridge University Press, 2014).

4 Achille Mbembe, *Necropolitics*. Trans. Steven Corcoran (Durham, NC: Duke University Press, 2019), p. 12.

5 W. E. B. Du Bois, *Darkwater: Voices from within the Veil* (Mineola: Dover Publications, 1999), p. 36.

6 Frank B. Wilderson, "Blacks and the master/slave relation" (2015), in Frank B. Wilderson et al., *Afro-Pessimism: An Introduction* (Minneapolis: Racked & Dispatched, 2017), pp. 20–1.

7 James Ferguson, *Global Shadows: Africa in the Neoliberal*

World Order (Durham, NC: Duke University Press, 2006), p. 204.

8 Vitally Lubin, "Libye, Mauritanie, partout dans le monde ... Stop à l'esclavage des Noirs," *Negus*, 4, December 2017, pp. 9–10.

9 Ajari, *Dignity or Death*, pp. 159–65.

10 Goldberg, *Are We All Postracial Yet?* p. 42.

11 Michelle Alexander, *The New Jim Crow: Mass Incarceration in the Age of Colorblindness* (New York: The New Press, 2012), pp. 6–7.

12 Didier Fassin, *L'ombre du monde: une anthropologie de la condition carcérale* (Paris: Seuil, 2017), p. 130. See also Assa Traoré and Geoffroy de Lagasnerie, *Le combat Adama* (Paris: Stock, 2019).

13 Men account for 93.2% of the incarcerated population in the United States, 34.8% of whom are Hispanic, 34.5% Black, 27.1% white, and 3.6% of other ethnicities: Federal Bureau of Prison Statistics as of February 25, 2017.

14 Jamie Grierson, "More than half of young people in jail are of BME background," *The Guardian*, Jan. 28, 2019.

15 Keeanga-Yamahtta Taylor, *From #Blacklivesmatter to Black Liberation* (Chicago: Haymarket Books, 2016), p. 129.

16 Jackie Wang, *Carceral Capitalism* (South Pasadena, CA: Semiotext(e), 2018), pp. 22–3.

17 Achille Mbembe, *Critique of Black Reason*. Trans. Laurent Dubois (Durham, NC: Duke University Press, 2017), p. 27.

18 Frank B. Wilderson III, S. Spatzek, and P. Von Gleich, "'The inside–outside of civil society': an interview with Frank B. Wilderson III," *Black Studies Papers*, 2, 1, 2016, p. 7.

19 Malcolm X, *Two Speeches by Malcolm X*. Ed. Betty Shabazz (New York: Pathfinder Press, 2011), p. 15.

20 Kwame Ture and Charles V. Hamilton, *Black Power: The Politics of Liberation* (New York: Vintage Books, 1967), p. 5.

21 Charles W. Mills, *The Racial Contract* (Ithaca, NY: Cornell University Press, 1997), p. 3.

22 Shelby, *We Who Are Dark*, pp. 11–12.

23 Kehinde Andrews, *Back to Black: Black Radicalism for the 21st Century* (London: Zed Books, 2018), p. 163. Andrews' emphasis.

24 Sexton, "The social life of social death: on Afro-pessimism and Black optimism," p. 28.

25 *Ibid.*, pp. 17–18.

26 Enrique Dussel, *1492: l'occultation de l'autre*. Trans. Christian Rubel (Paris: Éditions Ouvrières, 1992); Tzvetan Todorov, *La conquête de l'Amérique: la question de l'autre* (Paris: Seuil, 1982).

27 Patterson, *Slavery and Social Death*.

28 Jared Sexton, "Affirmation in the dark: racial slavery and philosophical pessimism," *The Comparatist*, 43, 2018, p. 91.

29 Wilderson III, *Afropessimism*, p. 218. Wilderson's emphasis.

30 Jared Sexton, *Black Men, Black Feminism: Lucifer's Nocturne* (London: Palgrave, 2018), p. 82.

31 Wilderson III, *Red, White & Black*, pp. 339–40.

32 *Ibid.*, p. 21.

33 Ferdinand de Saussure, *Course in General Linguistics*. Trans. Roy Harris (Chicago and La Salle, IL: Open Court, 2000), p. 118. Translation modified.

34 Judith Butler, *Gender Trouble: Feminism and the Subversion of Identity* (New York: Routledge, 2007), p. 24.

35 Adopting a Hegelian perspective on this point, rather than a structuralist or poststructuralist one, the philosopher Charles Mills developed a definition of humanity *in contradistinction to* the condition of free humanity and subjugated subhumanity, arguing, in reference to Orlando Patterson, that "freedom has been generated from the experience of slavery, that the slave establishes the norm for *humans*": Mills, *The Racial Contract*, p. 58.

36 Charles W. Mills, *Blackness Visible: Essays on Philosophy and Race* (Ithaca, NY: Cornell University Press, 1998), p. 6.

37 David Livingstone Smith, *Less than Human* (New York: St. Martin's Press, 2011), p. 101.

38 *Ibid.*, p. 101.

39 *Ibid.*, p. 25. Smith's emphasis.

40 David Livingstone Smith, *On Inhumanity: Dehumanization and How to Resist it* (New York: Oxford University Press, 2020), p. 19.

41 Frantz Fanon, *Black Skin, White Masks*. Trans. Richard Philcox (New York: Grove Press, 2008), p. 95. Translation modified.

42 Wilderson III, *Afropessimism*, p. 162.

43 *Ibid.*, p. 92.

44 David Marriott, *Haunted Life* (New Brunswick, NJ: Rutgers University Press, 2007), pp. 203–4.

45 David Marriott, *On Black Men* (Edinburgh University Press, 2000), p. 82.

46 *Ibid.*, p. 11. Marriott's emphasis.

47 Sexton, *Black Men, Black Feminism*, p. 84.

3 From the Black Man as Problem to the Study of Black Men

1 Christina Sharpe, *In the Wake: On Blackness and Being* (Durham, NC: Duke University Press, 2016), p. 74. Sharpe's emphasis.

2 Zakiyyah Iman Jackson, *Becoming Human: Matter and Meaning in an Antiblack World* (New York University Press, 2020), p. 4.
3 C. Riley Snorton, *Black on Both Sides: A Racial History of Trans Identity* (Minneapolis: University of Minnesota Press, 2017); Marquis Bey, *The Problem of the Negro as a Problem for Gender* (Minneapolis: University of Minnesota Press, 2020).
4 Marriott, *Haunted Life*, p. 2.
5 Philipp Dray, *At the Hands of Persons Unknown: The Lynching of Black America* (New York: The Modern Library, 2003); Amy Louise Wood, *Lynching and Spectacle: Witnessing Racial Violence in America, 1890–1940* (Chapel Hill: University of North Carolina Press, 2009).
6 Marriott, *On Black Men*, p. 10.
7 David Marriott, *Whither Fanon?* (Stanford University Press, 2018), pp. 70–1.
8 Zakiyyah Iman Jackson, "Waking nightmares," *GLQ: A Journal of Lesbian and Gay Studies*, 17, 2–3, 2011, p. 358.
9 Sexton, *Black Men, Black Feminism*, p. 57.
10 Curry, *The Man-Not*, p. 200.
11 Wilderson III, *Red, White & Black*, p. 311.
12 *Ibid.*, p. 332.
13 Curry, *The Man-Not*, pp. 150–1.
14 *Ibid.*, p. 6. Curry's emphasis.
15 Alford Young Jr., *Are Black Men Doomed?* (Cambridge: Polity, 2018), p. 11.
16 William A. Smith, "Toward an understanding of Black misandric microaggressions and racial battle fatigue in historically white institutions," in E. M. Zamani-Gallaher and V. C. Polite (eds.), *The State of the African-American Male* (East Lansing: Michigan State University, 2012), p. 266.
17 Sandor Ferenczi, Karl Abraham, and Sigmund Freud, *Psychoanalysis and the War Neuroses*. Ed. Ernest Jones (London, Vienna, and New York: The International Psychoanalytical Press, 1921).
18 William A. Smith, Tara J. Yosso, and Daniel G. Solórzano, "Challenging racial battle fatigue on historically white campuses: a critical race examination of race-related stress," in R. D. Coates (ed.), *Covert Racism: Theories, Institutions, and Experiences* (Leiden: Brill, 2011), p. 213.
19 Tommy J. Curry, "Killing boogeymen: phallicism and the misandric mischaracterization of Black males in theory," *Res Philosophica*, 95, 2, 2018, p. 235.
20 Sylvia Wynter, *No Humans Involved: An Open Letter to My Colleagues* (Publication Studio Hudson, 2015), p. 4. Wynter's emphasis.
21 *Ibid.*, p. 25. Wynter's emphasis.

22 Frantz Fanon, *The Wretched of the Earth*. Trans. Richard Philcox (New York: Grove Press, 2004), p. 13.
23 Wynter, *No Humans Involved*, p. 30. Wynter's emphasis.
24 G. W. F. Hegel, *Phenomenology of Spirit*. Trans. A. V. Miller (Oxford University Press, 1977), p. 117.
25 Curry, *The Man-Not*, p. 2.
26 Curry, "Killing boogeymen," p. 239.
27 George G. M. James, *Stolen Legacy: The Greeks Were Not the Authors of Greek Philosophy, but the People of North Africa, Commonly Called the Egyptians* (Mansfield Center, CT: Martino Publishing, 2015).
28 Cornel West, *Prophecy Deliverance!* (Louisville, KY: Westminster John Knox Press, 2002), p. 47.
29 Mills, *Blackness Visible*, p. 2. Mills' emphasis.
30 Tommy J. Curry, *Another White Man's Burden: Josiah Royce's Quest for a Philosophy of White Racial Empire* (Albany: State University of New York Press, 2018), p. 39.
31 Curry, *The Man-Not*, p. 141.
32 Curry, *Another White Man's Burden*, p. 131.
33 *Ibid.*, p. 19.
34 Tommy J. Curry, "Concerning the underspecialization of race theory in America: how the exclusion of Black sources affects the field," *The Pluralist*, 5, 1, 2010, p. 47.
35 Curry, *Another White Man's Burden*, p. viii.
36 Qtd. in Livingstone Smith, *Less than Human*, p. 161.
37 Peter Trawny, *Heidegger and the Myth of a Jewish World Conspiracy*. Trans. Andrew J. Mitchell (University of Chicago Press, 2016).
38 Stéphane Domeracki, *Heidegger et sa solution finale* (Saint-Denis: Connaissance et Savoirs, 2016).
39 Curry, "Concerning the underspecialization of race theory in America," p. 50.
40 Curry, *Another White Man's Burden*, p. xii.
41 Tommy J. Curry, "Will the real CRT please stand up? The dangers of philosophical contributions to CRT," *The Crit*, 2, 1, 2009, p. 27.
42 Curry, "Canonizing the Critical Race artifice," pp. 352–3.
43 Curry, "Will the real CRT please stand up?" pp. 45–6.
44 Curry, *Another White Man's Burden*, p. ix.
45 Curry, *The Man-Not*, p. 68.
46 *Ibid.*, p. 207.
47 *Ibid.*, p. 8.
48 Maxime Cervulle, *Dans le blanc des yeux: diversité, racisme et médias* (Paris: Éditions Amsterdam, 2013).
49 Judith Butler, *Senses of the Subject* (New York: Fordham University Press, 2015), p. 192.
50 Fanon, *Black Skin, White Masks*, p. xii.
51 Curry, "Killing boogeymen," p. 236.

52 Djamila Ribeiro, *La place de la parole noire*. Trans. Paula Anacaona (Paris: Anacaona Éditions, 2019), p. 37.
53 Curry, *The Man-Not*, p. 34.
54 Traoré and de Lagasnerie, *Le combat Adama*, p. 120.
55 *Ibid.*, p. 83.
56 *Ibid.*, p. 82.
57 Curry, *The Man-Not*, p. 176.
58 Curry, "Killing boogeymen," p. 265.
59 Andrews, *Back to Black*, p. 131.
60 bell hooks, *Yearning: Race, Gender, and Cultural Politics* (London: Routledge, 2015), p. 63.
61 bell hooks, *We Real Cool: Black Men and Masculinity* (London: Routledge, 2004), p. 54.
62 Fanon, *Black Skin, White Masks*, pp. 120–1.
63 Curry, *The Man-Not*, p. 55.
64 *Ibid.*, p. 142.
65 *Ibid.*, p. 172.
66 *Ibid.*, p. 120.
67 Curry, "Killing boogeymen," p. 245.
68 Dána-Ain Davis, "Obstetric racism: the racial politics of pregnancy, labor, and birthing," *Medical Anthropology*, 38, 7, 2019, pp. 560–73.
69 Sexton, *Black Men, Black Feminism*, p. 86.
70 Loretta J. Ross and Rickie Solinger, *Reproductive Justice: An Introduction* (Berkeley: University of California Press, 2017), p. 18.

4 A Politics of Antagonisms

1 Fanon, *Black Skin, White Masks*, p. 117.
2 Sexton, *Black Men, Black Feminism*, p. 83.
3 Frank B. Wilderson III, "The Black Liberation Army and the Paradox of Political Engagement," in Sabine Broek and Carsten Junker (eds.), *Postcoloniality–Decoloniality–Black Critique: Joints and Fissures* (Frankfurt: Campus Verlag, 2014), p. 177.
4 For a more thorough discussion of Rousseau and alienation from an Afropessimist perspective, see Ajari, *Dignity or Death*, pp. 186–7.
5 Aimé Césaire, *Toussaint Louverture: la revolution française et le problème colonial* (Paris: Présence Africaine, 1981), p. 33.
6 Qtd. in P. G. R., "L'esclavage au Canada," *Bulletin des Recherches historiques*, 2, 5, 1896, p. 73. See also Marcel Trudel, *L'esclavage au Canada français: histoire et conditions de l'esclavage* (Quebec: Presses Universitaires Laval, 1960), p. 55; and David Eltis, *The Rise of African Slavery in the Americas* (Cambridge University Press, 2000), p. 17.

7 Edmund Bailey O'Callaghan, *Documents Relative to The Colonial History of the State of New York*, vol. X (Albany, NY: Weed, Parsons & Company Printers, 1858), p. 210.
8 Warren, *Ontological Terror*, p. 76.
9 Karen E. Fields and Barbara J. Fields, *Racecraft: The Soul of Inequality in American Life* (London: Verso, 2012).
10 Eltis, *The Rise of African Slavery in the Americas*, p. 15.
11 Wilderson III et al., "'The inside–outside of civil society,'" p. 16.
12 Wilderson III, *Red, White & Black*, p. 141.
13 *Ibid.*, p. 77.
14 Hartman, *Scenes of Subjection*, p. 65.
15 Wilderson III, *Afropessimism*, p. 305.
16 Wilderson III, *Red, White & Black*, p. 337.
17 Isabelle Garo, *Communisme et stratégie* (Paris: Éditions Amsterdam, 2019), p. 16.
18 Patricia Hill Collins, *Black Feminist Thought: Knowledge, Consciousness, and the Politics of Empowerment* (New York: Routledge Classics, 2009), p. 309.
19 Cornel West, "American progressivism reoriented," in *The Cornel West Reader*, p. 332.
20 Curry, *The Man-Not*, p. 105.
21 Wilderson III, *Afropessimism*, p. 40. See also Curry, *The Man-Not*, p. 105.
22 Antoni Gramsci, *Selections from the Prison Notebooks*. Ed. and trans. Quentin Hoare and Geoffrey Nowell Smith (London: ElecBook, 1999), p. 642.
23 Ernesto Laclau and Chantal Mouffe, *Hegemony and Socialist Strategy: Towards a Radical Democratic Politics* (London and New York: Verso, 2001), p. 93.
24 Ernesto Laclau, *On Populist Reason* (London and New York: Verso, 2005), p. 74.
25 Laclau and Mouffe, *Hegemony and Socialist Strategy*, p. 91.
26 Norman Ajari, "Populisme de gauche et conscience noire: race, histoire et pluralisme après Laclau et Mouffe," *Philosophiques*, 48, 1, 2021, pp. 93–114.
27 Frank B. Wilderson III, "Gramsci's Black Marx: whither the slave in civil society?" *Social Identities*, 9, 2, 2003, p. 237.
28 Lawrence Grossberg, "On postmodernism and articulation: an interview with Stuart Hall," *Journal of Communication Inquiry*, 10, 2, 1986, p. 53.
29 Stuart Hall, "Old and new identities, old and new ethnicities," in David Morley (ed.), *Stuart Hall: Essential Essays Vol. 2* (Durham and London: Duke University Press, 2019), p. 79.
30 *Ibid.*, p. 80.
31 It should be mentioned that the visual arts have also seen a return of the question of Blackness. The era of Hall's overblown pride in minor Black differences has run its course. The cinema

of Jordan Peele or Ava DuVernay, the documentary films of Arthur Jafa or television series such as Little Marvin's *Them*, whatever their merits, all demonstrate the importance for contemporary filmmakers and artists of foregrounding Black positionality and the haunting experience of extreme violence suffered by the diaspora.

32 Wilderson III, *Red, White & Black*, p. 57.

33 *Ibid.*, p. 313.

34 David Austin, *Fear of a Black Nation: Race, Sex, and Security in Sixties Montreal* (Toronto: Between the Lines, 2013), p. 148.

35 Asad Haider, *Mistaken Identity: Race and Class in the Age of Trump* (London: Verso, 2018), p. 76.

36 Taylor, *From #Blacklivesmatter to Black Liberation*. This book's explanation of the origins of the Black Lives Matter movement is valuable, but its solutions, still driven by a romantic view of a diverse leftist coalition, as well as its functionalist interpretation of anti-Blackness, are problematic.

37 Curry, *The Man-Not*, p. 194.

38 Haider, *Mistaken Identity*, p. 37.

39 *Ibid.*, p. 35.

40 In a famous speech given in 1964, Malcolm X aptly described the animosity white people have toward Black aspirations for political separation and autonomy: "Segregation means that [the white man] puts you away from him, but not far enough for you to be out of his jurisdiction; separation means you're gone. And the white man will integrate faster than he'll let you separate" – Malcolm X, "The ballot or the bullet," BlackPast. org, July 26, 2010. This same problem has arisen in all the national contexts where there have been aspirations for a Black movement. See Aimé Césaire, "Lettre à Maurice Thorez, secretaire général du Parti communiste français," in *Écrits politiques: 1935–1956* (Paris: Jean-Michel Place, 2016); Steve Biko, *I Write What I Like: Selected Writings*. Ed. C. R. Aelred Stubbs (University of Chicago Press, 2015).

41 Haider, *Mistaken Identity*, pp. 15–16.

42 Wilderson III et al., "'The inside–outside of civil society,'" p. 18.

43 *Ibid.*, p. 18.

44 Wilderson III, *Afropessimism*, p. 171. Wilderson's emphasis.

45 Jesse McCarthy, "On Afropessimism," *Los Angeles Review of Books*, July 20, 2020.

46 Bryan Burrough, *Days of Rage: America's Radical Underground, the FBI, and the Forgotten Age of Revolutionary Violence* (New York: Penguin Books, 2015).

47 Huey P. Newton, *Revolutionary Suicide* (New York: Penguin Books, 2009).

48 Warren, *Ontological Terror*, p. 172.

49 Wilderson III et al., "'The inside–outside of civil society,'" pp. 18–19.
50 William L. Patterson (ed.), *We Charge Genocide: The Crime of Government against the Negro People* (New York: International Publishers, 1970).
51 Wilderson III, "Gramsci's Black Marx," pp. 238–9.
52 Carl Schmitt, *The Nomos of the Earth*. Trans. G. L. Ulmen (New York: Telos Press Publishing, 2003), p. 70. Schmitt's emphasis.
53 J. Sakai, *Settlers: The Mythology of the White Proletariat from Mayflower to Modern* (Montreal: Kersplebedeb, 2014), p. 5.
54 *Ibid.*, p. 8.
55 Dalie Giroux, "Husserl, Mishima et les avions: sens du déracinement à l'ère industrielle," *Sociétés*, 114, 2011, p. 129.
56 Dalie Giroux's notions regarding the intersection of place and thought appear to derive from Gilles Deleuze and Félix Guattari: these ideas are expressed in strikingly similar terms in the first part of *What Is Philosophy?*. In *Dignity or Death*, I addressed the problems with interpreting the stakes of African philosophy from their "geophilosophical" perspective: Ajari, *Dignity or Death*, p. 137.
57 Glen Sean Coulthard, *Red Skin, White Masks: Rejecting the Colonial Politics of Recognition* (Minneapolis: University of Minnesota Press, 2014), p. 61.
58 Wilderson III, *Red, White & Black*, p. 181.
59 Austin, *Fear of a Black Nation*, p. 7.
60 Wilderson III, *Red, White & Black*, p. 169.
61 Dalie Giroux, *Parler en Amérique: oralité, colonialisme, territoire* (Montreal: Mémoire d'encrier, 2018), p. 61.
62 Dalie Giroux, "Ce contre quoi il faut s'organiser," preface to Jackie Wang, *Capitalisme Carcéral* (Montreal: Éditions de la rue Dorion, 2020), p. 14.
63 Austin, *Fear of a Black Nation*, p. 40.
64 Robyn Maynard, *Policing Black Lives: State Violence in Canada from Slavery to the Present* (Halifax and Winnipeg: Fernwood Publishing, 2017), p. 5.
65 Wilderson III, *Red, White & Black*, p. 297.
66 *Ibid.*, p. 150.
67 Eduardo Viveiros de Castro, "The un-volunteers of the Fatherland." Trans. Rahul Bery. *Specimen: The Babel Review of Translations*, July 2, 2019: www.specimen.press/articles/os-involuntarios-da-patria.
68 Arturo Escobar, *Sentir-penser avec la terre: une écologie au-délà de l'Occident*. Trans. L'Atelier la Minga (Paris: Seuil, 2018), p. 102.
69 David Austin, *Fear of a Black Nation*, p. 36.
70 Dalie Giroux, *L'oeil du maître* (Montreal: Mémoire d'encrier, 2020), p. 52.

71 Wilderson III et al., "'The inside–outside of civil society,'" p. 14.
72 Giroux, *L'oeil du maître*, p. 126.
73 Jared Sexton, "The *vel* of slavery: tracking the figure of the unsovereign," *Critical Sociology*, 42, 4–5, 2016, p. 585.
74 Darryl Leroux, *Distorted Descent: White Claims to Indigenous Identity* (Winnipeg: University of Manitoba Press, 2019).
75 Giroux, *L'oeil du maître*, p. 18.
76 Pierre Vallières, *The White Niggers of America: The Precocious Autobiography of a Quebec Terrorist*. Trans. Joan Pinkham (New York and London: Monthly Review Press, 1971), p. 21.
77 Giroux, *L'oeil du maître*, p. 38.
78 *Ibid.*, p. 123.
79 *Ibid.*, p. 152.
80 One of the key points of this difference is that serfs were allowed to keep their family structure intact, which was not the case for slaves.
81 Ghassan Hage, *Is Racism an Environmental Threat?* (Cambridge: Polity, 2017), p. 32.
82 Austin, *Fear of a Black Nation*, p. 68.
83 Fanon, *Black Skins, White Masks*, p. 90.
84 Giroux, *L'oeil du maître*, p. 159.
85 *Ibid.*, p. 177.
86 *Ibid.*, p. 140.
87 Giroux, *Parler en Amérique*, p. 128.
88 Giroux, *L'oeil du maître*, p. 140.
89 Vallières, *Les Nègres blancs d'Amérique*, p. 371. *Translator's note*: This passage appears to be missing from the English translation cited above, which is why the French version is cited here. The translation is mine.
90 Austin, *Fear of a Black Nation*, p. 66.
91 Slavoj Žižek, *In Defense of Lost Causes* (London: Verso, 2009), p. 95.
92 Sexton, "The *vel* of slavery," p. 589.
93 Coulthard, *Red Skin, White Masks*, p. 13.
94 Achille Mbembe, "Afropolitanism," *Nka: Journal of Contemporary African Art*, 46, 2020, p. 60.
95 Wilderson III et al., "'The inside–outside of civil society,'" p. 7.
96 Charles W. Mills, *Black Rights / White Wrongs: The Critique of Racial Liberalism* (Oxford University Press, 2017); Domenico Losurdo, *Liberalism: A Counter-History*. Trans. Gregory Elliott (London: Verso, 2014).
97 Stuart Hall, "New ethnicities," in Kuan-Hsing Chen and David Morley (eds.), *Stuart Hall: Critical Dialogues in Cultural Studies* (London and New York: Routledge, 1996), p. 441.
98 *Ibid.*, p. 443.
99 Andrews, *Back to Black*, pp. 175–6.

100 Rachida Brahim, *La Race tue deux fois: une histoire des crimes racistes en France (1970–2000)* (Paris: Syllepse, 2020).

101 Abdellali Hajjat, *The Wretched of France: The 1983 March for Equality and against Racism*. Trans. Andrew Brown (Bloomington: Indiana University Press, 2022), p. 2.

102 The term *beur* is commonly used to refer to second-generation Maghrebi immigrants born in France. It is believed to derive from the word *Arab* (*arabe*) using a system of slang called *verlan*, in which syllables are inverted.

103 See Hajjat, *The Wretched of France*.

104 Norman Ajari, *La dignité ou la mort: éthique et politique de la race* (Paris: La Découverte, 2019), pp. 15–16. *Translator's note:* Although this book has been translated into English (*Dignity and Death*, cited above), this particular reference is only in the French edition.

105 Laurent Lévy, *"La Gauche," les Noirs et les Arabes* (Paris: La Fabrique, 2010), p. 52.

106 Talal Asad, *On Suicide Bombing* (New York: Columbia University Press, 2007).

107 Houria Bouteldja and Sadri Khiari (eds.), *Nous sommes les Indigènes de la République* (Paris: Éditions Amsterdam, 2012), p. 21.

108 Étienne Balibar, "Sujets ou citoyens? Pour l'égalité" (1984), in *Les frontières de la démocratie* (Paris: La Découverte, 1992), p. 63.

109 Étienne Balibar, "La société Métissé" (1984), in *Les frontières de la démocratie*, p. 77. See also Norman Ajari, "Human sciences as a battlefield: the reception of *Race, Nation, Class* in France," in Manuela Bojadžijev and Katrin Klingan (eds.), *Balibar/Wallerstein's "Race, Nation, Class": Rereading a Dialogue for Our Times* (Berlin: Argument Verlag, 2018), p. 24.

110 Lévy, *"La Gauche," les Noirs et les Arabes*, p. 140.

111 Sidi Mohamed Barkat, *Le corps d'exception: les artifices du pouvoir colonial et la destruction de la vie* (Paris: Éditions Amsterdam, 2005), pp. 23–4.

112 Sadri Khiari, "Construire une organisation politique autonome anticolonialiste" (2007), in *Nous sommes les Indigènes de la République*, p. 237. See also Sadri Khiari, *Pour une politique de la racaille: immigré-e-s, indigènes et jeunes de banlieues* (Paris: Textuel, 2006), p. 102.

113 Khiari, "Construire une organisation politique autonome anticolonialiste," p. 241; Khiari's emphasis.

114 Wilderson III et al., "'The inside–outside of civil society,'" p. 18.

115 Houria Bouteldja, *Whites, Jews, and Us: Toward a Politics of Revolutionary Love*. Trans. Rachel Valinsky (Cambridge, MA: MIT Press, 2017), pp. 55–6.

116 *Ibid.*, p. 67.
117 Jared Sexton, "The world love jam," *The Immanent Frame*, June 20, 2018: https://tif.ssrc.org/2018/06/20/the-world-love-jam.
118 Karen Brodkin, *How Jews Became White Folks & What That Says about Race in America* (New Brunswick: Rutgers University Press, 1998).
119 Leonard Saxe et al., *American Jewish Population Estimates 2020 Summary & Outlines* (Waltham, MA: Brandeis University, 2021).
120 Associated Press, "Dallas sniper profile: Micah Johnson was sent home from Afghanistan," *The Guardian*, July 9, 2016.
121 Fanon, *Black Skin, White Masks*, p. 95. Translation modified. See also Wilderson III et al., "'The inside–outside of civil society,'" p. 12.
122 Fanon, *Black Skin, White Masks*, p. 101. Translation modified.
123 Wilderson III, *Red, White & Black*, p. 38.
124 Enzo Traverso, *The End of Jewish Modernity*. Trans. David Fernbach (London: Pluto Press, 2016), p. 92.
125 Judy Malz, "'Cleansed by the Torah': why these Afrikaners converted to Judaism and moved to Israel," *Haaretz*, Sept. 30, 2021.
126 Sadri Khiari, "L'indigène discordant" (2005), in *Nous sommes les Indigènes de la République*, pp. 70–1.
127 Samia Errazzouki, "Between the 'yellow-skinned enemy' and the 'black-skinned slave': early modern genealogies of race and slavery in Sa`dian Morocco," *The Journal of North Africa Studies*, 2021, p. 6.
128 *Ibid.*, pp. 4–5.
129 *Ibid.*, p. 8.
130 Mercedes Garcia-Arenal, *Ahmad al-Mansur: The Beginnings of Modern Morocco* (Oxford: Oneworld Publications, 2009), p. 109.
131 El Hamel, *Black Morocco: A History of Slavery, Race, and Islam*. Translation modified.
132 *Ibid.*, p. 104.
133 Edward W. Said, *Orientalism* (New York: Vintage Books, 1979), p. 105.
134 Sexton, "The world love jam," n.p.
135 Sadri Khiari, *Malcolm X: stratège de la dignité Noire* (Paris: Éditions Amsterdam, 2013), pp. 106–7.
136 Houria Bouteldja, *Whites, Jews, and Us: Toward a Politics of Revolutionary Love*, p. 26.
137 Houria Bouteldja and Sadri Khiari, "L'évolution en ciseaux des champs de l'antiracisme" (2012), in *Nous sommes les Indigènes de la République*, p. 361.
138 Crystal Marie Fleming, *Resurrecting Slavery: Racial Legacies and White Supremacy in France* (Philadelphia: Temple University Press, 2017), p. 32.

139 Étienne Balibar, "Algérie, France: une ou deux nations?" in *Droit de Cité* (1998) (Paris: Presses universitaires de France, 2002), p. 79.

140 Aimé Césaire, "Séance du 13 novembre 1975," in *Écrits politiques: discours à l'Assemblée Nationale, 1945–1983* (Paris: Jean-Michel Place, 2013), p. 218.

141 Collectif/Brigade anti-négrophobie, "Autopsie de la négrophobie: chronique d'une mort annoncé," 2013, pp. 34–5.

142 As he has often repeated, Wilderson came to Marxism principally through Italian *operaismo*. He therefore may recall Mario Tronti's intriguing insight: "Knowledge is connected to the struggle. Whoever has true hatred has truly understood" – Mario Tronti, *Workers and Capital* (1966). Trans. David Broder (London: Verso, 2019), p. xviii.

Conclusion: Black Communism

1 Andrews, *Back to Black*, p. 56.

2 Annie Olaloku-Teriba, "Afro-pessimism and the (un)logic of anti-Blackness," *Historical Materialism*, 26, 2, 2018, p. 119.

3 *Ibid.*, pp. 110–11.

4 *Ibid.*, p. 113.

5 Kasereka Kavwahirehi, *Y'en a marre! Philosophie et espoir social en Afrique* (Paris: Karthala, 2018), p. 67.

6 Jared Sexton, *Amalgamation Schemes: Antiblackness and the Critique of Multiracialism* (Minneapolis: University of Minnesota Press, 2008), p. 40.

7 Karl Marx, *Capital (Vol. 1: A Critique of Political Economy)*. Trans. Samuel Moore, Edward Aveling, and Ernest Untermann (Overland Park: Digireads Publishing, 2017), p. 255.

8 Spillers, *Black, White and in Color*, p. 207.

9 Cedric J. Robinson, *Black Marxism: The Making of the Black Radical Tradition* (1983) (Chapel Hill: North Carolina Press, 2000), p. 171.

10 *Ibid.*, p. 10.

11 Huey P. Newton, "Intercommunalism" (1971), in *The Huey P. Newton Reader* (New York: Seven Stories Press, 2002), p. 184.

12 Kostas Axelos, *Héraclite et la philosophie* (Paris: Minuit, 1962); René Mouriaux, *La dialectique d'Héraclite à Marx* (Paris: Syllepse, 2010).

13 Philippe Lacoue-Labarthe, *Poetics of History: Rousseau and the Theater of Originary Mimesis*. Trans. Jeff Fort (New York: Fordham University Press, 2019).

14 James, *Stolen Legacy*; Yoporeka Somet, *L'Afrique dans la philosophie: introduction à la philosophie africaine pharaonique* (Paris: Présence Africaine, 2019).

15 Jacob Taubes, *Occidental Eschatology*. Trans. David Ratmoko (Stanford University Press, 2009).
16 Louis Althusser, *For Marx* (1969). Trans. Ben Brewster (London and New York: Verso, 2005).
17 Wilderson III, *Red, White & Black*, p. 80; Wilderson III, "Biko and the problematic of presence," in Andile Mngxitama, Amanda Alexander, Nigel C. Gibson (eds.), *Biko Lives! Contesting the Legacies of Steve Biko*, (New York: Palgrave Macmillan, 2008), p. 111.
18 Olaloku-Teriba, "Afro-pessimism and the (un)logic of Blackness," p. 96; Thomas, "Afro-Blue Notes," p. 304.
19 Édouard Glissant, *Caribbean Discourse: Selected Essays* (1989). Trans. J. Michael Dash (Charlottesville: University of Virginia Press, 1999), p. 15.
20 Jean-Luc Mélenchon, "La Créolisation n'est pas un projet ou un programme, c'est un fait," *L'Obs*, Sept. 25, 2020.
21 Wilderson III et al., "'The inside–outside of civil society,'" p. 8.
22 Sexton, "The *vel* of slavery," p. 593.
23 Marcus Garvey, *Philosophy and Opinions: Volume II* (New York: The Universal Publishing House, 1926), p. 70.
24 Rinaldo Walcott, *On Property: Policing, Prisons, and the Call for Abolition* (Windsor: Blioasis, 2021), p. 14.
25 *Ibid.*, p. 94.
26 Biko, *I Write What I Like*, p. 50.
27 Ajari, *Dignity or Death*, p. 104.
28 Biko, *I Write What I Like*, p. 51.
29 Richard Wright, *Black Power: Three Books from Exile – Black Power; The Color Curtain; and White Man, Listen!* (1954) (New York: HarperCollins, 2008). See also Yves Benot, *Idéologies des indépendances africaines* (Paris: Maspero, 1969), and Paul Gilroy, *The Black Atlantic: Modernity and Double-Consciousness* (Cambridge, MA: Harvard University Press, 1993).

Postface: The Conceptual Limitations of Studying Blackness

1 Robert Staples, "Race and colonialism: the domestic case in theory and practice," *The Black Scholar* 7, 9, 1976, pp. 37–49.
2 Sylvia Wynter, "No humans involved: an open letter to my colleagues," *Voices of the African Diaspora* 8, 2, 1992, pp. 13–18.
3 Tommy J. Curry, "Disaggregating death: George Floyd and the significance of Black male mortality in police encounters," in George Yancy (ed.), *Black Men from Behind the Veil:*

An Ontological Interrogation (Washington, DC: Lexington Books, 2021), pp. 65–79.

4 Tommy J. Curry, "He never mattered: poor Black males and the dark logic of intersectional invisibility," in Michael Cholbi, Alex Madva, Benjamin Yost, and Brandon Hogan (eds.), *The Movement for Black Lives: Philosophical Perspectives* (Oxford University Press, 2021), pp. 59–89.

5 Jennifer A. Hartfield, Derek M. Griffith, and Marino A. Bruce, "Gendered racism is a key to explaining and addressing police-involved shootings of unarmed Black men in America," *Inequality, Crime, and Health among African American Males: Research in Race and Ethnic Relations*, 20, 2019, pp. 155–70.

6 See E. Ashby Plant, Joanna Goplen, and Jonathan W. Kunstman, "Selective responses to threat: the roles of race and gender in decisions to shoot," *Personality and Social Psychology Bulletin*, 37, 9, 2011, pp. 1274–81; Andrew Todd, Kelsy C. Thiem, and Rebecca Neel, "Does seeing faces of young Black boys facilitate the identification of threatening stimuli?" *Psychological Science*, 27, 2016, pp. 384–93.

7 See Patrick Bayer and Kerwin Kofi Charles, "Divergent paths: a new perspective on earnings differences between Black and white men since 1940," *The Quarterly Journal of Economics*, 133, 3, 2018, pp. 1459–501; and Raj Chetty et al., "Race and economic opportunity in the United States: an intergenerational perspective," *The Quarterly Journal of Economics*, 135, 2, 2020, pp. 711–83.

8 Sharon D. Jones-Everly et al., "Premature deaths of young Black males in the United States," *Journal of Black Studies*, 51, 3, 2020, pp. 251–72.

9 See Raul Caetano, S. Ramisetty-Mikler, and C. A. Field, "Unidirectional and bidirectional intimate partner violence among white, Black, and Hispanic couples in the United States," *Violence and Victims*, 20, 4, 2005, pp. 393–406; and Carolyn West, "Partner abuse in ethnic minority and gay, lesbian, bisexual, and transgender populations," *Partner Abuse*, 3, 3, 2012, pp. 336–57.

10 M. Cascardi and S. Avery-Leaf, "Gender differences in dating aggression and victimization among low-income, urban middle school students," *Partner Abuse*, 6, 4, 2015, pp. 383–402.

11 Kathleen C. Basile et al., "Prevalence of intimate partner reproductive coercion in the United States: racial and ethnic differences," *Journal of Interpersonal Violence*, 36, 21–2, 2019, NP12324-NP12341.

12 See Tommy J. Curry and Ebony A. Utley, "She touched me: five snapshots of adult violations of young Black boys," *Kennedy Institute of Ethics Journal*, 28, 2, 2018, pp. 205–41; and Sharon G. Smith et al., *The National Intimate Partner and Sexual Violence Survey (NISVS): 2010–2012 State Report* (Atlanta,

GA: National Center for Injury Prevention and Control, Centers for Disease Control and Prevention, 2017): www.cdc. gov/violenceprevention/pdf/NISVS-StateReportBook.pdf.

13 Catherine G. Velopulos et al., "Comparison of male and female victims of intimate partner homicide and bidirectionality – an analysis of the national violent death reporting system," *The Journal of Trauma and Acute Care Surgery*, 87, 2, 2019, pp. 331–6.

14 See Tommy J. Curry, "Decolonizing the intersection: Black Male Studies as a critique of intersectionality's indebtedness to subculture of violence theory," in Robert Beshara (ed.), *Critical Psychology Praxis: Psychosocial Non-Alignment to Modernity/Coloniality* (Advances in Theoretical and Philosophical Psychology Series) (New York: Routledge, 2021), pp. 132–54; "Reconstituting the object: Black Male Studies and the problem of studying Black men and boys within gender theory," in Shirley Ann Tate (ed.), *Palgrave Handbook on Critical Race and Gender* (New York: Palgrave MacMillan, in press); and "Disaggregating death," pp. 65–79.

15 Sylvia Wynter, "Towards the sociogenic principle: Fanon, identity, and the puzzle of conscious experience, and what it is like to be 'Black,'" in Antonio Gomez-Moriana and Mercedes Duran-Cogan (eds.), *National Identities and Sociopolitical Changes in Latin America* (New York: Routledge, 2001), pp. 30–66.

16 Curry, *The Man-Not*, p. 4.

17 Derrick Bell, *Gospel Choirs: Psalms of Survival in an Alien Land Called Home* (New York: Basic Books, 1997), p. 23.

18 Mills, *Blackness Visible*, p. 4.

19 Ibid., p. 6.

20 Warren, *Ontological Terror*, p. 2.

21 Sylvia Wynter, "On how we mistook the map for the territory, and reimprisoned ourselves in our unbearable wrongness of being, of *Désêtre*: Black Studies toward the human problem," in Lewis R. Gordon and Jane A. Gordon (eds.), *Not Only the Master's Tools: African-American Studies in Theory and Practice* (Boulder: Paradigm Publishers, 2006), pp. 107–72.

Index

Nazism
  role of in Heidegger's work
    77–8
Négritude 11, 123–4, 131,
    161–2
neocolonialism 24
Newton, Huey 159
Nicholas V, Pope 44
Nkrumah, Kwame 24, 165
Noah 44
nomology/nomological 115,
    117
nomos 114–15, 116
North Africa
  anti-Arab racism 149
  dehumanization of Black
    people in 144
  humanity of 145
  slavery 144
North Africans 144–5
  and anti-Blackness 142–4
  divide between Blacks and
    139–41
  linking of anti-Blackness to
    slavery 140–1
Nyerere, Julius 165

Obama, Barack 16, 108, 109
Olaloku-Teriba, Annie 153,
    154–5, 156, 161
ontological antagonisms 98–9,
    100
ontological exile 128
ontology/ontologists
  gender 69
  paradigmatic 31, 55
  political 53–4, 58, 69, 96,
    100, 106, 117, 151
optimists 15

Pan-Africanism 12, 14, 23,
    114, 148, 158–9
paradigm 17, 29–36

of the slave 17, 33–4, 40,
    49, 55
  three steps constructing a 33
paradigmatic ontology 31, 55
Pathosformeln 30
patriarchy 85–6
  and Black feminism 85, 86–7
  and Black Male Studies 86–8,
    90–1
  and Black men 85–91
Patterson, Orlando 34
phallicism
  definition 84
  emergence of Black Male
    Studies and the critique of
    80–5
Philo of Alexandria 44
philosophy 75–8, 176
  ahistoricism of 76
  and biological racism 77–8
  dismissal of Black
    nationalism 78, 80
  Eurocentric and universalist
    view of reason 174
  ignoring of Black men in
    75–7
  lack of specialization on race/
    racism 78–9
  and pseudological criticism
    175
  race as social construct belief
    79
  structuring of by
    anti-Blackness and racism
    75–80
phobogenesis 67
Pinkney, Alphonso
  The Myth of Black Progress
    12
Point, Le 5
police violence, anti-Black
    92–3, 170
political liberalism 12